Animal
Rights

POINT //////
\\\\\\\|| COUNTERPOINT

Animal Rights

Kevin Hile

SERIES CONSULTING EDITOR
Alan Marzilli, M.A., J.D.

CHELSEA HOUSE
PUBLISHERS
An imprint of Infobase Publishing

Animal Rights

Chelsea House
An imprint of Infobase Publishing
132 West 31st Street
New York NY 10001

ISBN-10: 0-7910-7922-8
ISBN-13: 978-0-7910-7922-5

Library of Congress Cataloging-in-Publication Data

Hile, Kevin.
    Animal rights/by Kevin Hile.
        p. cm.—(Point-counterpoint)
Includes bibliographical references and index.
    ISBN 0-7910-7922-8
    1. Animal rights—Juvenile literature. [1. Animal rights.] I. Title.
II. Point-counterpoint.
HV4708.H55 2003
179'.3—dc22   2003023905

You can find Chelsea House on the World Wide Web at
http://www.chelseahouse.com

Text and cover design by Keith Trego

Printed in the United States of America

Bang 21C 10 9 8 7 6 5 4 3 2

This book is printed on acid-free paper.

CONTENTS

Introduction
Alan Marzilli, M.A., J.D.
Durham, North Carolina

The debates presented in POINT/COUNTERPOINT are among the most interesting and controversial in contemporary American society, but studying them is more than an academic activity. They affect every citizen; they are the issues that today's leaders debate and tomorrow's will decide. The reader may one day play a central role in resolving them.

Why study both sides of the debate? It's possible that the reader will not yet have formed any opinion at all on the subject of this volume—but this is unlikely. It is more likely that the reader will already hold an opinion, probably a strong one, and very probably one formed without full exposure to the arguments of the other side. It is rare to hear an argument presented in a balanced way, and it is easy to form an opinion on too little information; these books will help to fill in the informational gaps that can never be avoided. More important, though, is the practical function of the series: Skillful argumentation requires a thorough knowledge of *both* sides—though there are seldom only two, and only by knowing what an opponent is likely to assert can one form an articulate response.

Perhaps more important is that listening to the other side sometimes helps one to see an opponent's arguments in a more human way. For example, Sister Helen Prejean, one of the nation's most visible opponents of capital punishment, has been deeply affected by her interactions with the families of murder victims. Seeing the families' grief and pain, she understands much better why people support the death penalty, and she is able to carry out her advocacy with a greater sensitivity to the needs and beliefs of those who do not agree with her. Her relativism, in turn, lends credibility to her work. Dismissing the other side of the argument as totally without merit can be too easy—it is far more useful to understand the nature of the controversy and the reasons *why* the issue defies resolution.

The most controversial issues of all are often those that center on a constitutional right. The Bill of Rights—the first ten amendments to the U.S. Constitution—spells out some of the most fundamental rights that distinguish the governmental system of the United States from those that allow fewer (or other) freedoms. But the sparsely worded document is open to interpretation, and clauses of only a few words are often at the heart of national debates. The Bill of Rights was meant to protect individual liberties; but the needs of some individuals clash with those of society as a whole, and when this happens someone has to decide where to draw the line. Thus the Constitution becomes a battleground between the rights of individuals to do as they please and the responsibility of the government to protect its citizens. The First Amendment's guarantee of "freedom of speech," for example, leads to a number of difficult questions. Some forms of expression, such as burning an American flag, lead to public outrage—but nevertheless are said to be protected by the First Amendment. Other types of expression that most people find objectionable, such as sexually explicit material involving children, are not protected because they are considered harmful. The question is not only where to draw the line, but how to do this without infringing on the personal liberties on which the United States was built.

The Bill of Rights raises many other questions about individual rights and the societal "good." Is a prayer before a high school football game an "establishment of religion" prohibited by the First Amendment? Does the Second Amendment's promise of "the right to bear arms" include concealed handguns? Is stopping and frisking someone standing on a corner known to be frequented by drug dealers a form of "unreasonable search and seizure" in violation of the Fourth Amendment? Although the nine-member U.S. Supreme Court has the ultimate authority in interpreting the Constitution, its answers do not always satisfy the public. When a group of nine people—sometimes by a five-to-four vote—makes a decision that affects the lives of hundreds of millions, public outcry can be expected. And the composition of the Court does change over time, so even a landmark decision is not guaranteed to stand forever. The limits of constitutional protection are always in flux.

These issues make headlines, divide courts, and decide elections. They are the questions most worthy of national debate, and this series aims to cover them as thoroughly as possible. Each volume sets out some of the key arguments surrounding a particular issue, even some views that most people consider extreme or radical—but presents a balanced perspective on the issue. Excerpts from the relevant laws and judicial opinions and references to central concepts, source material, and advocacy groups help the reader to explore the issues even further and to read "the letter of the law" just as the legislatures and the courts have established it.

It may seem that some debates—such as those over capital punishment and abortion, debates with a strong moral component—will never be resolved. But American history offers numerous examples of controversies that once seemed insurmountable but now are effectively settled, even if only on the surface. Abolitionists met with widespread resistance to their efforts to end slavery, and the controversy over that issue threatened to cleave the nation in two; but today public debate over the merits of slavery would be unthinkable, though racial inequalities still plague the nation. Similarly unthinkable at one time was suffrage for women and minorities, but this is now a matter of course. Distributing information about contraception once was a crime. Societies change, and attitudes change, and new questions of social justice are raised constantly while the old ones fade into irrelevancy.

Whatever the root of the controversy, the books in POINT/ COUNTERPOINT seek to explain to the reader the origins of the debate, the current state of the law, and the arguments on both sides. The goal of the series is to inform the reader about the issues facing not only American politicians, but all of the nation's citizens, and to encourage the reader to become more actively involved in resolving these debates, as a voter, a concerned citizen, a journalist, an activist, or an elected official. Democracy is based on education, and every voice counts—so every opinion must be an informed one.

———•————————•————————•———

Since the dawn of history, humankind has depended upon other animals for survival: meat for food, fur for warmth, and labor for transportation and agriculture. However, many people have begun to view this relationship as one of exploitation, pointing out that people can survive on a vegetarian diet and wear clothing made of synthetic materials. Even worse, they say, are activities such as circuses and hunting, which use animals for entertainment and sport. At the same time, humans are coming up with new uses for animals, such as for biomedical research, a use that has facilitated some important discoveries. While many people deny that animals should have any "rights" beyond protection from abuse, some activists believe that animals *should* have many of the same rights as people. This volume examines the conflict in viewpoints among animal rights activists, people who support the traditional use of animals for food and clothing, the animal entertainment industry, and proponents of medical research on animals.

Author's Note

The subject of animal rights is multifarious. It encompasses disciplines ranging from bioethics and politics to economics, religion, and the law. While delving into the research for this book, I realized that it would be impossible to write it in such a way that it would cover all the many facets of the issue to everyone's satisfaction. Therefore, the reader should look to this publication as a good beginning overview on animal rights and not the final word on the subject. Within these pages I have endeavored to cover all of the central concepts that touch on animal rights; should the reader wish to explore the subject further, I have provided a list of books and organizations in the back of the book for further study.

Although there are, indeed, several other books that discuss the modern animal rights movement, what makes this book particularly unique is that it devotes much more attention to arguments against animal rights than most of the other works I've seen. It is my hope that *Animal Rights* will therefore open readers' eyes to the possibilities of both sides of the issue. Armed with a more balanced perspective, readers will be able to make better personal decisions about animal rights.

I would like to thank the following people for taking time out of their busy schedules for the interviews published in *Animal Rights:*

- Susan Bilsky, President of the Michigan Greyhound Connection

- Andrew Butler, International Lecturer for People for the Ethical Treatment of Animals

- Fred Jacobs, Senior Director of Communications at Busch Gardens Entertainment Corp.

- Kay Johnson, Vice President of the American Agricultural Alliance

- Ron Kagan, Director of the Detroit Zoological Institute and Society

- Crystal Miller-Spiegel, Outreach Director for the American Anti-Vivisection Society

- Dan Murphy, Vice President for Public Affairs at the American Meat Institute

- Barbara Pflughaupt, National Representative for Ringling Brothers

- The Reverend William Renfrew, Deacon at St. Paul's Episcopal Church, Lansing, Michigan

- Nathan Runkle, Director of Mercy for Animals

- Mike Severino, Ingham County, Michigan, Commissioner

- Mary Stid, Ingham County, Michigan, Commissioner

- Frankie Trull, President of the Foundation for Biomedical Research

The Debate Over Animal Rights

A Local Debate Reflects National Concerns

On a sunny day in May in the town of Mason, Michigan, a group of protesters gathered on the green lawn in front of the Ingham County Courthouse. Many of them were accompanied by pet dogs of various breeds; others, wisely, carried signs with pictures of their pet cats rather than bringing cats to a gathering where dozens of dogs were congregating. Some signs declared that the protester had rescued an otherwise unwanted pet from the local shelter; others protested directly against the sale of shelter animals for research. On the stairs, a microphone was set up and two Ingham County commissioners, John Nevin of the Fourteenth District and Mike Severino of the Fifteenth, who had organized the rally, stepped up to speak. They explained the need for public support against a policy they found abhorrent: the sale of abandoned cats and dogs from the county pound to Class B dealers, who obtain the animals they sell from various sources, rather than breeding the animals themselves.[1] These animals were then destined to be sold at a profit to university scientists for medical research.

> • **If you had a dog or cat that you couldn't keep anymore for one reason or another, would you be willing to have your pet used in a medical experiment that could lead to the creation of an important drug? What if the pet belonged to someone you didn't know?**

At the time, Ingham was one of only eight counties in Michigan that still allowed the sale of animals to Class B dealers, and the pet owners gathered at the rally fervently believed that research conducted on animals was inhumane and that the practice should not be supported by their tax dollars. On the other side of the argument, a majority of the county's commissioners, as well as the director of the county pound, explained that only a very few pets (47 animals in 2002) were sold to Class B dealers, and then only when all other options for finding them homes had run out. To put this into context, in 2002, there were 8,521 animals taken in by the shelter. Of these, 1,927 had been found homes and 1,433 had been euthanized (put to death painlessly). The commissioners in the majority reasoned that selling a few dozen animals at about ten dollars each to Class B dealers would bring some much-needed money to the shelter and also aid in medical research; these animals would have been euthanized anyway, the commissioners argued, so it wasn't as if they were killing animals that could have been adopted out. As Mark Grebner, an Ingham County commissioner from East Lansing, debates, "Is it better to destroy unwanted animals, or allow some to be used in veterinary or medical research? The animal rights activists mislead people into believing our choice is research versus adoption into loving homes."[2]

> • Some animals that are sent to shelters have handicaps, such as a missing leg, blindness, or deafness. Many of the Ingham County commissioners argued that these pets stood no chance of finding a home, so it was okay to send them to medical research facilities. Do you think shelters should not make extraordinary efforts to find homes for handicapped animals? Should only healthy animals be found homes?

But Commissioner Mike Severino said there was more going on at the shelter than most people knew about. Not only were there options for finding these animals homes, he maintained, but the animals weren't even being given a chance in the first place. He insists:

> What the written policy is is often different from what actually is being followed or executed. . . . The board of commissioners had a written policy that this is the pecking order in terms of how you're supposed to get rid of the animal: Your first effort is supposed to be reuniting [the animals] with their owner, and then setting them up for adoption. The reality was completely different. I mean, we have documented cases of animals being sold to research even before they were eligible for being adopted. And then for [the other commissioners] to argue that no one wanted to adopt these animals so we had to sell them to research, that's a fraud on the public.[3]

Fourteen of the sixteen commissioners on the board strongly supported allowing the sales to Class B dealers to continue. Severino and Nevin wondered why the other commissioners refused to ban a policy that brought so little money to the shelter. Severino even suspected that more than the number of animals on public record were actually being sold, making it possible for some officials to earn money under the table. "I don't have any evidence to substantiate that," he cautions, "but generally in these situations, I mean, not trying to cast any aspersions, but if you follow the money you usually find your answer."[4]

With continued public pressure being put on them, the commissioners eventually backed down, and on June 10, 2003, they signed a resolution banning the sale of animals from the Ingham County shelter to Class B dealers. Severino and Nevin were pleased. Although they knew this would not put an end to the use of dogs and cats in research entirely (universities can still buy animals directly from the shelter), their main goal had been to stop their local government from being involved. Not everyone was happy with the results, though. Three commissioners—Mary Stid, Mark Grebner, and Debbie DeLeon—dissented from the decision. As Severino and Nevin suspected that the commissioners and county pound were misleading the public, Stid, for one, felt that animal rights activists had also been less than honest about how research causes pain for cats and dogs:

> They pull [information] on research done on rats and monkeys and everything else into cats and dogs. And primarily what we are aware of in our cats and dogs going to Michigan State [University] or the University of Michigan [is that] many of those animals—I'm not saying all, because I don't know, but I have been to the facility—many of those animals are used for veterinarians' surgeries. So the animal is anesthetized, goes in for the surgery, and then is euthanized. They don't suffer agony or pain; they don't feel it. And that helps veterinarians be good veterinarians to take care of the wanted pets. I'm very disturbed that they [animal rights groups] have spent so much time and money when they should be using it for spaying and neutering programs.[5]

Stid, who once suffered from a pancreatic illness that nearly killed her, feels that she and numerous others have benefited from medical research performed on animals. "If you've ever had a blood transfusion you have used animal research because all of the work done with blood and transfusions came from animals," she noted, adding that animal rights advocates will not

More dealers, fewer inspections

The Puppy Protection Act, part of a Senate-approved overhaul of farm programs, would toughen the rules governing dog breeding. Some 3,400 licensed breeders of dogs and other animals across the nation are currently inspected at least once a year by the Department of Agriculture, which only regulates breeders whose puppies are sold through pet stores.

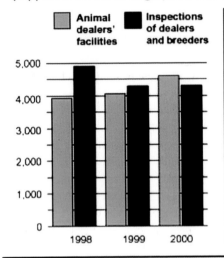

	Animal dealers' facilities	Inspections of dealers and breeders

Breeders by state

States with the highest number of breeding licenses

Missouri	1,092
Oklahoma	423
Kansas	410
Iowa	311
Arkansas	185
Nebraska	145
Pennsylvania	126
South Dakota	95
Texas	87
Minnesota	81

SOURCE: USDA Animal Welfare Report, 2000

AP

In response to the protests of animal rights activists about conditions in the dog breeding industry, the government has, over a period of several years, enacted legislation to try to better protect the welfare of animals. However, because the government does not regulate all categories of breeders, animal rights activists complain that many facilities are going unchecked.

stop with Class B dealers. "Their ultimate goal is no animal research, period."[6] That final step, if attainable, is many years away. In the meantime, the debate in Ingham County has inspired Senator Valde Garcia of Livingston County to introduce Senate bills 542 and 543 in Lansing. The aim of the bills is to establish even more regulations against animals being used in research laboratories.

The Ingham County debate illustrates only two issues—how we deal with the problems of unwanted dogs and cats and the ways in which we conduct medical research—in the far larger debates on animal rights. Even so, it clearly demonstrates how differing opinions on animal rights can ignite fiery passions.

What Do Animals Mean to Us?

Human beings owe a great deal to animals. Not only have they been a source of food and clothing, but for thousands of years, they have served as a labor force, pulling wagons, plows, chariots, and early fire engines. Animals are an integral part of every culture on the planet, appearing in our myths, legends, fables, superstitions, songs, and modern literature. Dogs, cats, and other species are our companions, comforting us when we are alone or sick, or when we simply wish to go on a walk or relax with a game of catch. In more recent times, they have been used extensively in medical research, helping to develop drugs through scientific experiments that have, in some cases, become extremely controversial. It's safe to say that humanity would not be what it is today if it were not for animals.

> • **Animals are an important part of every culture on our planet. How might human societies be different if animals were not part of our history, agriculture, literature, and music?**

Yet despite the many obvious advantages of having animals in our lives, the relationship between human beings and animals has been a checkered one. At times, animals have been exalted. In the days of the ancient Egyptian pharaohs, cats were worshiped as gods; in modern-day India, it is still forbidden to eat or harm cattle, which are considered holy. In North America, many Native American tribes revere and honor animals such as the wolf, eagle, and bison. A less well-known example comes from the island of Madagascar. Here, sifaka lemurs were once thought to be the incarnation of the native people's sun-worshiping ancestors because of this animals' habit of sunning itself in a position that appears to imitate a meditating wise man.

But animals have been reviled over the ages, too. Cats were once believed to be the demonic familiars of witches. And who could forget that it was the devil in the form of a snake who tempted Eve with the apple from the Tree of Knowledge in the Garden of Eden? Superstitions and ignorance have led people to persecute many animal species. In the United States, for example, hunters once shot wolves until they almost became extinct, and the U.S. government paid bounties to these hunters to encourage the elimination of wolves. Similarly, prairie dogs have been regularly shot and poisoned by ranchers who complain that cattle break their legs by stepping in prairie dog holes. Today, wolves, prairie dogs, and other species are protected in America by laws such as the Animal Welfare Act of 1966 and the Endangered Species Act of 1973. These and other laws, both in the United States and abroad, are evidence that attitudes toward animals and how they should be treated have been changing in recent years.

> • **Human beings often kill predatory animals, such as wolves and lions, on sight. Today, there are many laws protecting these and other species. Although people aren't dependent on these species for survival, why might they still be important to us? Would it matter if, for example, wolves became extinct?**

Early Attitudes Toward Animals

For the majority of the history of Western civilization, animals have been viewed as tools and resources to benefit humanity. This was considered ethical by most Christian theologians because animals were not believed to have souls and were thus not entitled to the same consideration as humans. The Book of Genesis in the Bible, it was argued, supported the view that animals were created by God to serve man. The Bible states: "And God said, Let us make man in our image, after our likeness:

and let them have dominion over the fish of the sea, and over the fowl of the air, and over the cattle, and over all the earth, and over every creeping thing that creepeth upon the earth."[7]

According to this reasoning, it was ethical to use animals for food, clothing, labor, or anything else human beings needed because God had given us the right to do whatever we wanted with all other living creatures. St. Thomas Aquinas (c. 1224–1274) further argued that animals would not go to heaven, since in heaven people would not need to eat, make clothes, or do any work, making animals unnecessary. On the other hand, St. Francis of Assisi (1181–1226), who is considered the patron saint of animals in the Roman Catholic Church, believed that all animals should be treated with compassion.

Later, with the rise of the Age of Reason in Europe during the eighteenth century, science began to take over the argument from theologians. Still, the conclusions drawn continued to favor humans over animals. Human beings, it was said, had intellect and could reason, whereas animals could not. Furthermore, it was believed that animals did not possess the capacity to suffer from pain the way people did. For these reasons, other species were not deserving of the same considerations given to people.

- **Some people believe in the theory of evolution, while others call themselves Creationists and believe that animals were created by God in their present forms. How might these different beliefs affect how people feel about the importance of animal life?**

Darwinism's Impact

An important shift in attitudes toward animals did not come until the nineteenth century, as new ideas and social movements began to change people's feelings about animals. One of the most influential events of this period was the publication of *The Origin of Species* (1859) by British naturalist Charles Darwin

(1809–1882), which argued that species evolve over time through natural selection. Natural selection is a process by which animals with certain physical or behavioral traits that are advantageous to their survival will manage to reproduce more successfully than other animals. Creatures without those traits will die off.

Darwin had formed his theories based on observations of animal life on the Galapagos Islands chain in the Pacific Ocean. He had traveled there aboard the H.M.S. *Beagle* in 1831, and observed that animals that appeared to have originated from the same species had developed certain physical adaptations that made them more suited to different island environments. Over time, this resulted in the rise of new species, while other species that were not as well adapted to their environment eventually became extinct.

The idea of evolution was not completely without predecessors. For example, Darwin's own grandfather, Erasmus Darwin (1731–1802), had discussed evolutionary principles in his *Zoonomia; or, The Laws of Organic Life* (1794), and Jean Baptiste Lamarck (1744–1829) proposed in 1801 that environmental pressures on animals could change their behaviors, and that changing behaviors could lead to changes in anatomical structures over time. He elaborated on this idea in his *Zoological Philosophy,* which was published in 1809. Lamarck was perhaps too far ahead of his time, however, and his theories were dismissed by his colleagues. Darwin's book, on the other hand, received much more attention and had a major impact on society.

Theologically, the theory of evolution was controversial because it contradicted the Bible, which says that animals were all created by God in the same form in which they exist today (this is sometimes referred to as Creationism). Sociologically speaking, the repercussions of Darwinism provided ammunition against compassion for animals. A contemporary of Darwin's, English philosopher Herbert Spencer (1820–1903), interpreted the idea of natural selection in terms of what he called "survival of the fittest." This led to Social Darwinism, which, among other things, argued that since human beings were on the top of the food chain, they were the most "fit" and therefore deserved to survive more than other animal species did.

This conclusion had not been Darwin's intention at all. Another, more positive outcome of his theory was the idea that other animals on the planet had more in common with humans than had previously been thought. This meant that they were deserving of more compassion. As Rod Preece and Lorna Chamberlain write in their book *Animal Welfare and Human Values*, "Darwin was . . . responsible for creating the intellectual climate in which humans would come to recognize their responsibilities to animals, not as was customary as a consequence of human benevolence to creatures different in kind but because such beings were in all relevant respects similar to ourselves."[8]

Animal Welfare Organizations and the Anti-Vivisectionist Movement

At the same time that scientific and philosophical ideas about animals' relationship to people were changing because of Darwinism, a new movement concerned with the welfare of domestic animals was on the rise. The early 1800s saw the beginnings of laws against cruelty toward animals in England. Laws against cockfighting, dog fighting, and the abuse of other domestic animals were passed. And in 1824, the Royal Society for the Prevention of Cruelty to Animals (RSPCA) was founded by Richard Martin (1754–1834). The ideals of the RSPCA were spread to the United States through the work of Henry Bergh (1811–1888), who founded the American Society for the Prevention of Cruelty to Animals (ASPCA) in 1866. The goal of these organizations was—and is—to ensure that pets and animals used for domestic purposes are treated humanely. By organizing various campaigns, the ASPCA has managed to get laws passed making it illegal to abuse or neglect animals such as dogs, cats, and farm animals.

Of particular concern to many of those in the growing

animal welfare movement was the use of animals in scientific experiments. Many of these animals were being operated on while still alive and without the benefit of anesthesia. This is known as "vivisection," and the people opposed to it were—and are—called Anti-Vivisectionists. The first society organized against vivisection was the Society for the Protection of Animals Liable to Vivisection, founded in England by Frances Power Cobbe (1822–1904). In 1883, Caroline Earle White (1833–1916), who had been active in the Pennsylvania chapter of the ASPCA and had headed its Women's Branch, founded the American Anti-Vivisection Society (AAVS). Although the ASPCA was also against vivisection, the AAVS focused on the issue exclusively.

The AAVS's efforts helped to pass some state laws banning the use of live animals for experiments in schools. Because its members were almost exclusively women, however, the AAVS became an easy target for critics in the age before feminism. Some scientists said the women in the group were overly emotional, to the point of hysteria, about the treatment of animals. The activists were considered well-meaning Christian women who nevertheless didn't understand why research on animals was so necessary. Because of such attitudes, the anti-vivisection movement faltered and died by the end of the nineteenth century.

A New Era of Animal Rights Activists

After the decline of the AAVS, the animal rights movement was relatively inactive until after World War II. The 1950s and 1960s, however, saw the founding of the Animal Welfare Institute in 1951, the Humane Society of the United States (HSUS) in 1954, the Friends of Animals in 1957, and the Fund for Animals in 1967, as well as many other local, national, and international organizations that are too numerous to list. These and other groups reenergized the fight to pass legislation for the humane treatment of animals. Some of the most significant federal laws to be passed at this time were the Humane Methods of Slaughter Act of 1958, which demanded that animals used for food be stunned or anesthetized before they were slaughtered, and the Laboratory Animal Welfare Act of 1966, which said that animals used for experiments must be provided with plenty of food, water, and clean living conditions, and that laboratories that worked with live animals must be licensed. The Laboratory Animal Welfare Act later became known as the Animal Welfare Act of 1970. The Act was revised in 1985 and again in 1990 to include regulations that address the need for more intelligent animals, like dogs and monkeys, to be provided with mental stimulation, such as toys to play with and human interaction, and physical exercise outside their cages.

THE LETTER OF THE LAW

Federal Animal Welfare Act and Regulations
2131. Congressional statement of policy

The Congress finds that animals and activities which are regulated under this chapter are either in interstate or foreign commerce or substantially affect such commerce or the free flow thereof, and that regulation of animals and activities as provided in this chapter is necessary to prevent and eliminate burdens upon such commerce and to effectively regulate such commerce, in order—

(1) to insure that animals intended for use in research facilities or for exhibition purposes or for use as pets are provided humane care and treatment;

(2) to assure the humane treatment of animals during transportation in commerce; and

(3) to protect the owners of animals from the theft of their animals by preventing the sale or use of animals which have been stolen.

The Congress further finds that it is essential to regulate, as provided in this chapter, the transportation, purchase, sale, housing, care, handling, and treatment of animals by carriers or by persons or organizations engaged in using them for research or experimental purposes or for exhibition purposes or holding them for sale as pets or for any such purpose or use.

Although such regulations were a move in the right direction, many people believed that they did not go far enough. In his famous 1975 book about animal rights, *Animal Liberation: A New Ethics for Our Treatment of Animals,* philosopher Peter Singer wrote that, although animals don't have the same intellectual capacity as humans, can't speak, and don't experience emotions the same way people do, their lives still have value. Singer, a utilitarian philosopher, weighs the issue of right and wrong in his book based on costs versus benefits. In the case of animal rights (Singer does not actually use the word *rights* because he believes that neither animals nor people intrinsically possess rights), the life of an animal is worth more than the benefits that people receive from activities that cause the animal harm. Another prominent contemporary philosopher, Tom Regan, who was an early advocate of vegetarianism, went further and declared that animals' lives do indeed have *intrinsic* value.[9] Together, Singer and Regan have been stalwart proponents for animal rights for the last several decades.

> • **Which is more important: the life of a human being or the life of a chimpanzee? How about the life of a human versus that of a dog? A human versus a squirrel? A human versus an ant?**

Animal Rights vs. Animal Welfare: What's the Difference?

It should be noted at this point that there is a distinction to be made between the terms *animal welfare* and *animal rights.* The former is concerned with the well-being of all animals and advocates that animals, especially those under human care, should be well fed, provided with medical attention when needed, and should never be subjected to physical or mental abuse. The ASPCA is a good example of an animal welfare organization. Animal rights groups, on the other hand, go a step further and say that animals should not be used at all for labor, agriculture, food, clothing, or entertainment. The most radical groups even argue against the use of animals as pets. In short, animal rights supporters believe that other species should be afforded the same considerations for life as people and should not be "enslaved" in cages of any kind. The most prominent of these animal rights groups in the United States today is People for the Ethical Treatment of Animals (PETA). As PETA explains on its Website, however, although animals deserve certain rights, this does not necessarily mean that they have the same rights as people in all cases:

> Animals have the right to equal consideration of their interests. For instance, a dog most certainly has an interest in not having pain inflicted on him or her unnecessarily. We therefore are obliged to take that interest into consideration and respect the dog's right not to have pain unnecessarily inflicted upon him or her.
>
> However, animals don't always have the same rights as humans, because their interests are not always the same as ours and some rights would be irrelevant to animals' lives. For instance, a dog doesn't have an interest in voting and therefore doesn't have the right to vote, since that right would be as meaningless to a dog as it is to a child.[10]

Generally speaking, there are few people in the United States today who are opposed to the idea that animals should be treated humanely. It is therefore with the more controversial concept of animal rights that this book will be concerned.

Animals Are Worthy of Certain Rights

It was not very long ago in the course of human history that various races and ethnic groups within our own species were considered inferior to people of European ancestry. Americans, of course, are well aware of the history of white people's treatment of African Americans, including centuries of enslavement and the denial of basic civil liberties even decades after blacks were officially emancipated. Women of all races were also discriminated against and were not allowed to vote until the addition of the Nineteenth Amendment to the Constitution in 1920. These rights were denied because those in power—white men, especially those who were landowners—considered other types of people inferior for various cultural, religious, economic, and political reasons. In fact, for many people, these prejudices continue today. Yet, in recent years, Americans for the most part have become enlightened enough to understand that we all belong to the human race, and we all deserve equal rights under the law. Might this consideration also be extended to all living things, and not just *Homo sapiens*?

- **Do you believe that the struggle for civil rights is comparable to the fight for the liberties of nonhuman species?**

Whites once considered African Americans a separate species not far advanced above "lower animals"; in another example of prejudice, women were once thought too emotional and not intelligent enough to be entrusted with the right to vote for government officials. Both notions, of course, are now widely considered ridiculous. Today, we have overcome many prejudices (though certainly not all!) that are based on race and gender, and we are in the midst of eliminating prejudices based on other factors, such as sexual orientation, because we are slowly recognizing that all people share a common humanity. Although no one is arguing for the right of animals to vote in elections, get married, or hold a job, what animal rights groups do propose is that the traits they feel nonhuman species share with us—consciousness, emotions, the ability to experience suffering—entitle them to the basic right to be free from the control of human beings. As Peter Singer writes in his book *Animal Liberation*:

> A liberation movement demands an expansion of our moral horizons. . . . We need to consider our attitudes from the point of view of those who suffer by them, and by the practices that follow from them. If we can make this unaccustomed mental switch we may discover a pattern in our attitudes and practices that operates so as consistently to benefit the same group—usually the group to which we ourselves belong—at the expense of another group.[1]

Animals are similar to people.

According to evolutionary theory, more intelligent animals, such as dolphins, gorillas, and humans, evolve over time from less advanced species that go all the way back to the first single-celled life-forms. If we go back far enough in time, we would find that all species connect to a single common ancestor. Depending on how closely we are related on the evolutionary family tree, some species have more genes in common than others. For example, biologists believe that the closest living relative to *Homo sapiens* is *Pan troglodytes,* commonly known as the chimpanzee. According to Morris Goodman of the Wayne State University School of Medicine, 99.4 percent of the genes in human beings are also present in chimpanzees. "We humans appear as only slightly remodeled chimpanzee-like apes,"[2] Goodman concludes about his recent study.

> • **Should the percentage of genes that humans have in common with other animals be used as a barometer for their entitlement to certain rights? For example, does an animal that shares 99 percent of our genes deserve more rights than one that only has 80 percent or 70 percent?**

With only a 0.6 percent difference in genetic makeup between a human and a chimp, certain questions arise: Couldn't an animal so similar to us share many of the same traits that make us human? And, if so, might they not deserve some of the same basic rights? Scholars used to believe that what separated humans from beasts was people's ability to use tools. This was proven to be an erroneous distinction when animal researcher Jane Goodall discovered chimpanzees fashioning and using tools in the wild. Since then, other animal species have been observed using tools: Egyptian vultures will use rocks to break open ostrich eggs; sea otters similarly use rocks to open oyster shells; and woodpecker finches will make tools out of cactus needles to extract grubs from tree branches. These are just a few examples. Animals can also perform other tasks analogous to human endeavors, including architecture (e.g., beavers building dams and wasps constructing nests that can actually be air-conditioned) and even agriculture (a species of ants has, in a sense, domesticated aphids for a milk-like substance they produce).

Animals have intelligence.

Humans might boast a large brain size, but brain volume in itself doesn't indicate intelligence with any accuracy. Whales, for example, have much larger brains than people, yet they are not generally considered equally intelligent; chimpanzee brains are also larger in proportion to their entire body mass than are the brains of humans, but, again, they are not considered as intelligent. On the other hand, whereas large brains don't always equal intelligence, some animals with much smaller brains have surprised scientists with their mental acuity. A good example of this is the African Grey parrot, which has a brain about the size of a walnut. In 1990, Dr. Irene M. Pepperberg of the Department of Ecology and Evolutionary Biology at the University of Arizona published a remarkable paper about the communication abilities of an African Grey parrot named Alex.[3] Most people know that parrots can imitate sounds and words very well, but scientists had been unsuccessful in showing that parrots can understand and participate in a meaningful dialogue before Pepperberg's work.

Pepperberg was able to demonstrate that parrots can use words as labels to properly identify objects, colors, and shapes; they can also use conjunctions, grasp concepts such as "absence" and "permanence," express desires verbally, and count (although she cautions that Alex the parrot might have just been very good at estimating numbers of objects and may not, in fact, have been counting). Her work with parrots has led Pepperberg to believe that parrots might think just like we do. Although their brains are smaller, they are able to process information in ways that are analogous to the workings of the human mind.

Better-known examples of animal communication involve experiments with apes using symbols or American Sign Language (ASL), the system of hand and arm gestures used by the hearing impaired to communicate. Some of the earliest experiments were conducted with chimpanzees. Drs. Allen and Beatrice Gardner, for instance, managed to train a chimp named Washoe to use some sign language during the late 1960s at the University of Oklahoma's Institute of Primate Studies. In another example, in research that was designed to develop ways to improve the communications skills of mentally handicapped children, Dr. Sue Savage-Rumbaugh, a Georgia State University professor at the Yerkes Regional Primate Center, has worked with chimpanzees, orangutans, and bonobos (a close relative of the chimp), training them over the last several decades to use a computer keyboard that allows them to synthesize spoken English. Koko, the now-famous lowland gorilla, has learned many words in ASL. Koko, who was born in 1971, has been the subject of years of study at the Gorilla Foundation in Woodside, California. According to the foundation's Website, "Koko has a working vocabulary of over 1,000 signs. Koko understands approximately 2,000 words of spoken English. Koko initiates the majority of conversations with her human companion and typically constructs statements averaging three to six words. Koko has a tested IQ of between 70 and 95 on a human scale, where 100 is considered 'normal.'"[4]

> • **Is language a good indication of intelligence? There are many ways that animals can communicate—with sounds, body language, and smells—that are not like human language. Should animal communication skills be judged based on how similar they are to human language?**

With the many similarities between higher apes and people, one might not be too surprised that chimps and gorillas can learn to communicate with humans, at least on a basic level. But should we define language ability exclusively in human terms? Animals, research has shown, have developed very complex forms of communication among themselves that suit their own needs very well. For example, according to a *Science World* article by Karen de Seve, "New research shows that prairie dogs use descriptive chirps to inform their colonies about predators and intruders—a human's size, for example, the colors he wears, how fast he's moving, even whether he's carrying a gun."[5] Even bees have developed an elaborate way of communicating the location and quantity of food using dance-like movements that are performed for other bees.

Animals do, indeed, seem capable of fairly sophisticated language. Does this mean they should be treated like people, though? After all, a robot can be programmed to act intelligently, but it is only a machine. This question brings us to animal emotions.

Animals may have emotions.

Perhaps a more difficult argument against the rights of animals is that they are not capable of experiencing feelings or emotions in the same way people do. Science has often reduced nonhuman species to biological machines that merely adapt and react according to instincts that have been programmed into them through inherited traits. Explanations for animal behavior are based on the idea that animals only do things that will help them or their offspring survive and thus perpetuate their genes to the next generation. Animals, the argument continues, favor passing along their own genes over those of another within their own species.

Many scientists caution against the hazards of anthropomorphism—projecting human traits, such as the ability to love, onto animals—and feel that all animal behavior can be better explained in unemotional terms. As psychoanalyst Jeffrey Moussaieff Masson writes in his book *When Elephants Weep:*

> Comparative psychology to this day discusses observable behavior and physical states of animals, and evolutionary explanations for their existence, but shies away from the mental states that are inextricably involved in that behavior. When such states are examined, the focus is on cognition, not emotion. The more recent discipline of ethology, the science

of animal behavior, with its insistence on distinctions between species, also seeks functional and causal, rather than emotive, explanations for behavior. The causal explanations center on theories of "ultimate causation"—the animal pairs [mates] because this increases reproductive success—as distinguished from "proximate causation"—the animal pairs because it has fallen in love. Although the two explanations are not necessarily mutually exclusive—one of the best-known figures of ethology, Konrad Lorenze, spoke confidently of animals falling in love, becoming demoralized, or mourning— the field as a whole has continued to treat emotions as unworthy of scientific attention.[6]

Yet time and again biologists and other researchers have seen human-like, often apparently emotional, behavior among animals. For example, animal researcher Jane Goodall, in her autobiography *Reason for Hope,* describes how her early observations of chimpanzees revealed their surprising similarities to humans:

[T]here were the postures and gestures that complemented the sounds they made—their communication repertoire. Many of these were common to human cultures around the world—kissing, embracing, holding hands, patting one another on the back, swaggering, punching, kicking, pinching, tickling, somersaulting, and pirouetting. And these patterns appeared in the same kind of contexts and seemed to have the same kind of meaning as they do for us. I gradually learned about the long-term affectionate and supportive bonds between family members and close friends. I saw how they helped and cared for each other. I also learned that they could bear grudges that could last for more than a week. I found that their society was complex.[7]

Goodall's observations were initially dismissed by biologists because she was not a formally trained scientist. Today, of course, she is considered a world authority on chimpanzees and their behavior. Emotions are not limited to chimps, however, as Masson has illustrated. *When Elephants Weep* includes numerous examples of animals of all types of species exhibiting everything from anger to affection. Do animals feel loneliness? Masson offers the example of beavers that, if not provided with a mate, will sometimes refuse to eat or move until they die. Can animals mourn the death of another? Masson describes an incident involving elephants:

> An observer once came across a band of African elephants surrounding a dying matriarch as she swayed and fell. The other elephants clustered around her and tried mightily to get her up. A young male tried to raise her with his tusks, put food into her mouth, and even tried sexually mounting her, all in vain. The other elephants stroked her with their trunks; one calf knelt and tried to suckle. At last the group moved off, but one female and her calf stayed behind. The female stood with her back to the dead matriarch, now and then reaching back to touch her with one foot. The other elephants called to her. Finally, she walked slowly away.[8]

Masson argues, too, that animals experience positive emotions, such as friendship, love, and joy. Chimps and gorillas in captivity have been given kittens as pets and appear to love and protect them; geese and eagles form lifelong bonds with their mates and often appear to grieve, sicken, and die when their mates die; river otters are famous for their love of play, often making slides out of snowy hillsides and playing on them for hours. Animal play, in fact, has been one activity that has been subject to much scientific inquiry. As Masson explains, scientists have proposed that "perhaps it is a form of practice, of learning to perform tasks; . . . or perhaps it exercises developing social, neurological, or physical capacities." Interaction between animals of the same species can help form social bonds and physical coordination, both beneficial in the struggle for survival. Masson also notes, however, that sometimes animals from different species play together, and that this has been observed both in captivity and in the wild. In one example, he tells of a dwarf mongoose that tried to make friends with a lizard in Kenya. It's hard to find a reason why the mongoose might think such behavior could help it survive. Might it just be playing with the lizard for the fun of it?

> • Do you believe animals can experience emotions, or are they just acting on instinct when they protect their young or appear to mourn for their dead?

The ideas of consciousness, self-awareness, and the soul may be applied to animals.

An even more complex concept to grasp than animal intelligence or emotions is whether animals are conscious and self-aware

Animal Faithfulness: The Story of Two Geese in Love

One morning many years ago, a farmer living near Buenos Aires witnessed the heart-rending tenacity of this love when he went riding on horseback and noticed on the plain ahead of him two geese, a white male and a brown female, walking in the distance. Drawing closer, he observed that the female was plodding steadily southward. The male, greatly agitated, walked about forty or fifty yards ahead of her, periodically rising into the air with forlorn cries. After flying a short way, the gander turned back to rejoin his mate in her weary march. This pattern was repeated again and again. The female had broken her wing and, unable to fly, had set forth afoot on her fall migration to the Magellanic Islands. Driven by his deepest instincts to fly south, the male nevertheless refused to abandon his partner. He remained loyal to her in her hour of need, plaintively begging her to spread her wings and join him in the long flight home. The pair was truly faithful "until death do us part."

Source: Gary Kowalski, *The Souls of Animals*, Walpole, NH: Stillpoint Publishing, 1991.

the way human beings are. According to the *Stanford Encyclopedia of Philosophy,*

> Two ordinary senses of consciousness which are not in dispute when applied to animals are the sense of consciousness involved when a creature is awake rather than asleep, or in a coma, and the sense of consciousness implicated in the basic ability of organisms to perceive and thereby respond to selected features of their environments, thus making them conscious or aware of those features. Consciousness in both these senses is identifiable in organisms [that] belong to a wide variety of taxonomic groups.[9]

What is more subject to debate is whether animals possess *self-consciousness,* or the ability of an animal to be aware of itself as an entity separate from its surroundings and other living creatures, to be aware that it is a unique being. Some studies seem to have shown that at least some animals possess this quality. Chimpanzees and bottlenose dolphins, for instance, are able to recognize themselves in a mirror and distinguish themselves as separate from others of their own kind. In the case of dolphins, self-consciousness was demonstrated in an experiment performed by Diana Reiss at the Wildlife Conservation Society in which the cetaceans' bodies were drawn on with odorless markers. After they were marked, the dolphins immediately swam to mirrors to check themselves out. Two reasons why this study was so significant are that, first, dolphins were the first non-primate species proven to have self-awareness, and, second, dolphins do not have frontal lobes in their brains. The mental activity that makes self-awareness in chimps and people possibly occurs in the forebrain, but since dolphins don't have a forebrain and can still recognize their own individuality, then it can no longer be asserted that a frontal lobe is a prerequisite for self-awareness. Perhaps, then, brain anatomy alone can't be used to make the argument that humans are the only species with an advanced consciousness.

> • **Is it possible to know for certain whether another animal— or even another human being—is self-aware without seeing through the other's eyes?**

Another aspect of consciousness is called the "theory of mind," which is defined as the ability to recognize that other creatures besides oneself have thoughts and feelings. In an article published in *Psychology Today*, Clive Wynne relates that recent experiments have shown that chimpanzees do possess theory of mind. Wynne describes one such experiment:

> [The chimpanzee] Sheba has been watching one trainer put food into one of four cups. She can't see which cup because they are hidden from her view—but she can clearly see that this trainer (we'll call him the "knower") had some food and put it in a cup. Now the knower comes back into the room together with another trainer (a "guesser"). If Sheba has a theory of mind—an awareness that the trainers have a conscious awareness of their own—she should know that the guesser did not see where the knower put the food.
>
> The two trainers are in the room. The knower points to a cup; the guesser points to a cup. The knower points to the cup into which he had placed food earlier; the guesser—well, he just guesses. What does Sheba do? She chooses the cup to which the knower points.[10]

Similarities between humans and the great apes (gorillas, chimps, bonobos, and orangutans) are considered now to be so striking that a group called the Great Ape Project has recently been pressing the United Nations to grant apes rights that will be internationally recognized.

The above examples seem to demonstrate that animals are intelligent, have feelings, and have other abilities similar to those of human beings. One point animal rights groups stress regarding these issues is that people can't say humans are more worthy than animals to live freely because of their intelligence, ability to speak, or other such factors. Such an argument can easily be turned around. For example, many mentally handicapped people have IQs that measure well below that of the average gorilla; a human infant lacks language skills; patients who are comatose are unable to express themselves at all; a homicidal criminal shows less compassion for other people than a faithful dog. Yet we don't judge such people to be unworthy of compassion and justice. Why, then, do we do so for animals?

Humans are not superior to animals.

Although members of the animal rights movement will not argue that animals are the equivalent of people in all ways, that is really not the issue for them. Instead, what they argue is that animals are more than just living machines that exist for us to use however we please. According to rights advocates, many people take the attitude that human beings are superior to other animals. The word that describes this attitude, first coined by Richard Ryder of the RSPCA in 1971, is *speciesism.* Speciesism is the viewpoint that human needs take priority over those of other species because we believe ourselves to be superior, even if to fulfill our needs means exploiting animals in ways that would be considered horrifying if exercised against people. Michael W. Fox, a veterinarian and vice president of the Humane Society of the United States, feels that speciesism is a symptom of modern society because of the beliefs that form the foundation of the American economic system. American capitalism, he writes in his 1990 book, *Inhumane Society: The American Way of Exploiting Animals,* is "driven by an ideology that has come to place economic interests and the iron law of supply and demand over the autonomy, intrinsic value, and interests of the individual, be it human or animal."[11]

• **Should attorneys be allowed to represent animals the same way they might represent a person who can't speak for him- or herself?**

Animal rights supporters point out that speciesism is just another form of racism and is no better than our history of prejudice against people of other races, ethnic groups, religions, and gender. One thing that distinguishes speciesism from other forms of prejudice, however, is that the victims—animals—can't speak for or defend themselves. Andrew Butler, international lecturer for People for the Ethical Treatment of Animals (PETA), explains the argument against speciesism this way:

> Animal rights isn't necessarily about loving animals or even liking animals. It's about something much more important than that. . . . It's really about fighting against prejudice; fighting against oppression wherever it occurs. It has many parallels with other social justice movements. What we're dealing with really is a form of prejudice. It's speciesism. Not valuing animals because we view them as somehow different and inferior, as unworthy of respect. It's the same sort of mind-set that has allowed the exploitation of others throughout the ages. It's what allowed the Holocaust to happen. It's what allowed Apartheid to take place in South Africa.
>
> But really it's just getting people to understand that animals are made of flesh and blood just as we are. They have the capacity to feel pain and stress just as we do, and for that alone animals are deserving of our respect and they shouldn't be treated just as meat-producing, milk-producing machines. They shouldn't be treated just as test tubes with tails. These animals have worth in and of themselves; they value their life; they care and nurture for their young; they build communities amongst themselves. If you look at the animal kingdom, they're architects, they're builders, they're fun seekers. It's not anthropomorphism, it's just simple common sense, simple observation that tells us this.
>
> So when we're talking about animal rights we're not talking

about the right to vote or to drive. That would be entirely use-
less to animals. But simply that we give equal consideration to
the needs of animals. . . . [They need a life] that is free, one
that they can live on their own terms.[12]

Another term animal rights groups use is *anthropocentrism,*
which is basically the belief that human beings think the world
revolves around them and that the world should be interpreted
only in human terms. This can be a dangerous philosophy that
will harm not only animals but humans as well. As Gary Kowalski
writes in *The Souls of Animals,* the negative effects might even rob
us of our spirituality:

> One might say that we "de-humanize" animals, but this would
> not be accurate, since animals are not human. Rather, we
> "de-sacralize" animals—rob them of their holy qualities—and
> in the process de-humanize ourselves. For animals cannot be
> relegated to the status of objects. When we treat them as if they
> were mere biological machines—collections of conditioned
> reflexes—we injure both their nature and our own.[13]

Even discounting the possibility that animals think, feel,
and perhaps have some kind of consciousness, the final question
for animal rightists is a moral one. British philosopher Jeremy
Bentham (1748–1832) is often quoted as summarizing this
position most succinctly: "The question is not, Can they reason?
nor, Can they talk? but, Can they suffer?"[14]

———————•————————•————————•———————

Because animals are extremely similar to human beings in a
number of ways, animal rights supporters argue that animals
should be granted certain rights, such as the right to life and
liberty, that are generally given to humans.

Animals Are Not Worthy of Rights Like Those of Humans

While current developments in animal research are indeed revealing more and more similarities between humans and other species, is it really only a matter of degree that separates the species? Philosophers have debated this issue repeatedly over the centuries. Aristotle (384–322 B.C.), for instance, asserted that animals exist for the sake of man.[1] Thomas Aquinas (c. 1224–1274) and René Descartes (1596–1650) are often cited as two famous thinkers of their respective times who felt that animals were inferior to humans—Aquinas because they lacked souls, Descartes because they could not think or experience emotions in the same way people do. The eighteenth-century philosopher Immanuel Kant (1724–1804) declared that animals are not self-conscious (actively aware of their own individuality) and exist "merely as a means to an end. That end is man."[2]

In the twenty-first century, progress in biology and animal

behavior sciences has made the boundaries between human and animal much fuzzier. Animal rights groups have been quick to note this in their arguments. "They point to science's inability to document absolute differences between human and beast," Tim Stafford writes in a *Christianity Today* article. "But this hardly suggests that we should treat animals well." Stafford reverses the pro–animal rights argument to reveal a flaw in its reasoning: "The animal-rights movement would like to raise animals to the moral status of humans. It would be just as *logical* to lower humans to the moral status of animals."[3] Some distinction must be made, then, between animals and humans, because it is unlikely that people will ever consider animals our moral equivalent. Still, the difficulty remains to define what distinguishes us from other species.

> • **If animals were granted legal rights to liberty and self-determination, might this in some way cheapen the value of rights possessed by people?**

The human brain is unique.

Michael Allen Fox, writing in his *The Case for Animal Experimentation: An Evolutionary and Ethical Perspective,* acknowledges the similarities between humans and animals, but goes on to assert that the differences are too pronounced to ignore. When it comes to the human brain, for example, he points out that brain size alone is not a reliable indication of intelligence. One must consider other factors, such as "the degree of convolution and thickness of the cortical surface (neocortex) and the overall density of cerebral neurons."[4] That is to say, the number of "wrinkles" in the human brain far exceeds that in other species, with the possible exception of some cetaceans. This creates more surface area and, consequently, more cerebral neurons, allowing for increased brain activity. In addition, brain mass—not just volume—must be considered. Fox refers to a study by Harry J. Jerison in which the scientist compared the brain weights of animals with comparable overall body weights. Using a formula he called the "encephalization quotient," Jerison found, according to Fox, that "the actual brain size of humans comes out to six times what should be expected of a typical comparable mammal."[5]

> • **How much should intelligence alone be a factor in determining the rights of a living creature?**

Human tool making and language are extremely sophisticated.

Fox continues to show significant differences between people and animals in the areas of tool making and language. Yes, he concedes, animals can make tools, but humans can design and build much more sophisticated tools because of our highly developed hands. A dolphin, despite its intelligence, couldn't build an automobile even if it knew how because it has flippers instead of hands. "The importance of this capacity cannot be overstated," says Fox, "for because of it sophisticated exploratory behavior, creative artistry/design, and technology become possible—in short, our species' adaptation to and high degree of formative influence upon its environment."[6] Adding to this advantage, human beings are the only animals on the planet to have made use of fire.

> • **Dolphins have been judged to be extraordinarily intelligent, yet they lack hands and fingers to build sophisticated tools. Should tool-making skills, then, be one way that human beings are judged to be unique and superior to other animals?**

Humans also are capable of much more advanced language than even the higher primates, such as chimpanzees. Chimps and other primates do not, for one thing, possess the anatomy to produce the wide variety of sounds that humans do; furthermore, their limited intelligence confines them to a vocabulary that does not exceed that of a typical two-year-old human child. Fox goes on to declare that many of the conclusions reached by researchers such as Sue Savage-Rumbaugh have led to misleading arguments about chimpanzees' abilities. "Unfortunately," writes Fox, "much of what has been reported about chimpanzees' language skills is inaccurate, leading to exaggerated claims by popularizers of this research."[7] Savage-Rumbaugh herself, states Fox, once admitted that early research methods had been defective and tainted by "an inherent bias toward a set of presumptions about the significance of symbol manipulation formerly reserved for children."[8] A big difference between human language capabilities and those of chimpanzees and gorillas is the ability to discuss objects and ideas that are not physically present (abstraction) and the ability to syntactically organize words into complex sentences. Humans are capable of both these skills, whereas animals, to our knowledge, are not.

The problem with trying to teach animals human language, say skeptics, is that language is an innately human (genetically inherited) trait developed over the ages to aid in human survival. To try to make an animal speak like a human being, therefore, makes about as much sense as trying to teach a person to fly or breathe underwater. We simply aren't designed to do so. In an article published in the London *Guardian*, Peter Jenkins wrote about the work that was being done with chimps by researchers at the University of Oklahoma. He noted that chimps were capable of responding "yes" or "no" to questions, expressing regret or gratitude, and making simple requests, such as asking for food or a toy, but could do nothing much more sophisticated than this. One might argue that the chimps' behavior is a form of crude language, but whether it is the equivalent of human language depends, as Jenkins and several chimp researchers point out, on one's definition of language. According to Jenkins, famous linguistics expert Noam Chomsky once concluded, "human language appears to be a unique phenomenon, without significant analogue in the animal world."[9]

Humans and animals are not morally equivalent.

Those who oppose the fundamental argument of animal rights groups that people's use of other animals for various purposes is immoral "speciesism" will sometimes point out that animals are often guilty of activities that most humans would consider highly disturbing and immoral. Life in the animal kingdom is far from an idyllic existence where each species treats the others with respect. Even within species, animals are guilty of what would be heinous crimes if perpetrated by human beings. For example, a male African lion will slaughter the cubs of other male lions in order to mate with the females of a pride so that they will bear his cubs instead. Animal rights groups have claimed that slaughterhouses where cattle are bludgeoned to death before being processed are inhumane. Yet is this more inhumane than what happens when a pack of wolves catches a deer, tearing into its flesh and eating it while it is still alive?

Animals, indeed, are capable of shocking behavior. In an article published in *Audubon* magazine, Richard Conniff provides some other examples. Noting one animal rights protester's admonition that all animals should be free, Conniff responds:

> I wondered if making every creature on Earth free meant that the speaker intended to restrain the copper-colored fly known as *Bufolucilia silvarum*, which deposits its eggs in the nostrils of toads and frogs. When the larvae hatch, they blind their hosts and devour them. In the interest of preventing needless slaughter, would she speak sternly to the great horned owl, which may decapitate fifteen adult common terns but eat just one? Would she admonish the mink, which is capable of wiping out whole muskrat families in a senseless killing frenzy? Would she issue sound dietary edicts to the bulimic Adélie penguin, which sometimes causes itself to vomit, the better to kill and consume more fish?[10]

It seems to opponents of animal liberation that such behavior on the part of other animal species is just as cruel—if not more so—as some of the acts that animal rights groups condemn people for performing on animals. Animals can be guilty of unnecessary killing, they murder members of their own species, they cause severe torture, and primatologists have even discovered that troops of chimpanzees will fight territorial wars in the wild. If the logic of animal rights groups against people's treatment of animals is that we are capable of more kindness than other species because we can stop ourselves from eating, wearing, and experimenting on animals, then could this not be seen as an implicit confirmation that human beings are, indeed, superior to other animals, which are unable to express such compassion?

> • **Animals in the wild might be more concerned with their own survival than how they treat other species. Does this justify how humans treat other species—since other animals kill for food and other reasons—or should human beings consider themselves morally superior and therefore be more compassionate to other animals?**

Anthropomorphism warps the concepts of pain and suffering.

Some people look at a pig in a pen and conclude that because it doesn't have room to roam freely, it must be suffering, because, after all, a human being would not wish to be held in a small cage. However, this argument assumes that pigs think and feel in the same way that human beings do. Researchers like those at the Center for Food Animal Productivity and Well-Being at Purdue University, for example, have suggested that sows may be perfectly content in a small, confined space while they are nursing their piglets and that there is no convincing evidence that such quarters cause the pigs any psychological distress.

The way an animal experiences pain is also subject to interpretation. It is a big leap in logic, say some, to conclude that because animals are physically capable of feeling pain, they are our emotional equivalents, making it immoral to, for example, kill them for food. Stephen Budiansky feels that this is simply not enough justification to change the current human-animal relationship:

> One of the reasons I fundamentally disagree with the animal-rights philosophy is that it seems to be based on the notion that pain is the overriding factor in determining whether an animal has rights. . . . The idea that because animals can suffer pain they therefore deserve equal consideration is a very limited view of the world. And even more than that, sentience or consciousness is not the same as a moral capacity, a capacity to anticipate the future, a capacity to have thoughts about thoughts, a capacity to have an awareness of oneself as an independent moral agent. These are things that result in different experiences of the world, and I think they make it perfectly valid and normal to make distinctions between us and other animals.[11]

Anthropomorphism

[Gr.,=having human form], in religion, conception of divinity as being in human form or having human characteristics. Anthropomorphism also applies to the ascription of human forms or characteristics to the divine spirits of things such as the winds and the rivers, events such as war and death, and abstractions such as love, beauty, strife, and hate. As used by students of religion and anthropology the term is applied to certain systems of religious belief, usually polytheistic. Although some degree of anthropomorphism is characteristic of nearly all polytheistic religions, it is perhaps most widely associated with the Homeric gods and later Greek religion. Anthropomorphic thought is said to have developed from three primary sources: *animism*, legend, and the need for visual representations of the gods.

Source: *The Columbia Encyclopedia*, 6th ed. New York: Columbia University Press, 2002.

Legal rights are for people, not animals.

The idea that animals do not have legal rights in human society goes back to the beginning of civilization. Animals have always been considered property, and although the law usually dictates that the owners of animals are entitled to compensation when someone damages or destroys their animals, the animals themselves do not have any rights in court. As D. G. Ritchie put it back in the nineteenth century, "If rights are determined solely by reference to human society, it follows that the lower animals, not being members of human society, cannot have rights."[12]

In more recent years, attitudes have changed somewhat, not only among the public, but in the courts as well. There is more of a sense that animals, legally speaking, lie somewhere between inanimate objects and human beings. Nevertheless, rulings have been based not upon how an animal itself has suffered but rather on how an animal's death or injury has affected its owner. Steven J. Bartlett, a senior research professor of philosophy at Oregon State University, comments on the Animal Law Website:

> In legal discourse, there has been a gradual increase in the number of cases in which the courts have ruled that an animal's value is not to be reduced and equated to property value. In parallel, there has been some increase in the number of successful claims for emotional distress for tortuous injury or killing of nonhuman animals. . . . In many of these cases, changes in human attitudes and laws relating to the legal thinghood of nonhuman animals appear to be taking place. However, we need to discern whether these cases truly represent changes in the property status of animals, or whether they instead merely reflect increasing judicial recognition of human sentiment. . . .
>
> The courts have sometimes been willing to take explicitly into account a companion animal's special value to the owner, and in so doing they continue a pattern of establishing value in homocentric terms. Seldom do courts consider nonhuman

animals as ends in themselves, with interests of their own. When attention has been directed in this way, it has been in discussions that seek to situate the legal status of nonhuman animals somewhere between property and legal personhood.[13]

Bartlett then summarizes that "the central legal issue in this context and at the present time is therefore simply put: 'Animals are not humans and are not inanimate objects. Presently, the law has only two clearly separated categories: property or juristic persons.'"[14] Because animals are not considered persons by the courts, they cannot sue for any damages done to them—even if they *could* speak. Animal rights advocates say that they take their cases to the courts precisely because animals are incapable of speaking on their own behalf. But they face an uphill battle, not only because other species are not considered juristic persons but also because the animal rights groups lack legal standing. In the case of *Lujan* v. *Defenders of Wildlife* in 1992, the Supreme Court held that in order to sue on behalf of endangered species, animal rights activists must:

> Submit affidavits or other evidence showing, through specific facts, not only that listed species were in fact being threatened by funded activities abroad, but also that one or more of the respondents' members would thereby be "directly" affected apart from their "'special interest' in th[e] subject."[15]

In simple terms, people cannot sue for the rights of animals, but only for their own rights; therefore, they must prove that an action harming animals causes some legally recognized form of damage directly to the person bringing the lawsuit.

Perhaps the closest rights advocates have come to proving that they had legal standing and, consequently, winning a case came in 1998 with the *Animal Legal Defense Fund* v. *Glickman* trial. Here, the ALDF sued Daniel Glickman, the secretary of the U.S. Department of Agriculture (USDA) at the time, for not setting strict enough laws for the treatment of animals in exhibits. This resulted in an "aesthetic injury" to the public viewing poorly treated primates at the Long Island Game Farm Park and Zoo. Although the judge in the case originally agreed that the plaintiff had legal standing in the matter, the final ruling was in favor of Glickman because the judge concluded that the USDA's regulations were consistent with the spirit of the Animal Welfare Act. As the final resolution of the *Animal Legal Defense Fund* v. *Glickman* case demonstrates, proving this type of direct legal damage can be difficult.

> • **Under U.S. law, the status of animals is somewhere between property and people. How can this fact be used to argue for or against animals' rights?**

While rights advocates are not seeking the equivalent legal status of humans for animals in all cases (for example, voting rights and driver's licenses), they do still seek the basic legal rights a person has to life and freedom. To grant these rights, however, the courts would have to recognize animals as persons, and this is what they have been unwilling to do. In addition to the general sentiment that human law is for human beings alone, those who oppose the animal rights movement do so because they feel that raising the status of animals would subsequently lower the status of human beings by denying that we have qualities that set us apart from other species. This would mean disregarding "innate human characteristics, the ability to express reason, to recognize moral principles, to make subtle distinctions, and to intellectualize."[16] As Joseph Lubinski explains, "The existence of rights, and the extension thereof, is a human debate; one in which, by definition, animals cannot have a voice."[17]

The overzealous demand for animal rights may lead to misanthropy.

Animal rights groups do not distinguish between humans and animals, and this is what frustrates many who oppose their viewpoint. A now somewhat infamous quote made by PETA president Ingrid Newkirk in 1983 is often used to represent how animal rightists feel about their fellow human beings: "[A]nimal liberationists do not separate out the human animal, so there is no rational basis for saying that a human being has special rights. A rat is a pig is a dog is a boy. They're all mammals." [18]

Some people have accused animal rights advocates outright of favoring animals over their own kind. For example, Edwin A. Locke, a psychologist and professor emeritus at the University of Maryland at College Park, has called PETA—and others in favor of animal rights—a group of misanthropes, or haters of humankind. Citing a number of statements made by PETA representatives, he says,

> The granting of fictional rights to animals is not an innocent error. We do not have to speculate about the motive, because the animal "rights" advocates have revealed it quite openly. Again from PETA: "Mankind is the biggest blight on the face of the earth"; "I do not believe that a human being has a right to life"; "I would rather have medical experiments done on our children than on animals." These self-styled lovers of life do not love animals; rather, they hate men. [19]

The moral issue involving animal versus human life is probably the most difficult to answer. Is animal life really equivalent to human life? If, for instance, the lives of a thousand children suffering from cancer could be saved by research that would result in the death of a thousand monkeys, would the sacrifice be ethical? Many people would say yes. As Frankie Trull, president of the Foundation for Biomedical Research, puts it:

> Animals are partners, and they have been since the beginning of time. Man's responsibility is to ensure that animals are treated humanely and responsibly. I think because the vast majority of us grew up with Mickey Mouse, sort of Disney

characters, and our pets, because we're such an urbanized society now as opposed to people who grew up in the olden days on farms, that we tend to anthropomorphize that animals have the same characteristics as people. Animals want to be cared for and housed properly; they want to be dry; they want to be in a reasonable environmental temperature; they want their food; they want their water. They don't need new clothes and they aren't people, but that doesn't mean we shouldn't treat them with respect, and the fact that scientists partner with animals in research is really a great privilege, and it needs to be addressed that way. But Man's greatest responsibility is to improve the quality of life of Man.[20]

Traditionally, animals have been seen as something expressly designed for the benefit of human beings. Those who oppose animal rights argue that animals cannot truly be compared to humans in terms of moral worth and the ability to reason.

Animals Should Not Be Used in Medical Research

The debate over the use of animals in medical and other types of scientific research and testing is a central issue in the battle for animal rights. It is what gave rise to the first large animal rights group in the United States, the American Anti-Vivisection Society, and it has been a major campaigning issue for many pro–animal rights organizations ever since. Using animals for medical research is a tradition that can be traced back almost 2,500 years to the days of ancient Greece. "The first recorded use of animal experimentation," according to Jordan Curnutt in his *Animals and the Law: A Sourcebook*, "occurred in about 450 B.C.E. when Alcmaeon of Croton severed the optic nerve of a dog, and noted that blindness resulted."[1] Such experimentation continued throughout the development of Greek and Roman civilization. This was long before the creation of anesthesia, so animals were never given anything to ease their pain, and since these early scientists often wished to observe the functions of a living body in action, the animals were usually not killed before procedures were performed. The fall of Rome and the onset of the Dark Ages in around the fifth century A.D. saw such experimentation disappear in Europe. However, it was revived with the Italian Renaissance in the 1500s and 1600s as scientific inquisitiveness flourished once again.

> • **Does the fact that animal experimentation has been going on for centuries justify its continuation? Why or why not?**

To say that early scientists were unconcerned that their work inflicted pain on animals would not be entirely accurate, though. Many, if fact, found such work repulsive, yet they maintained that it was necessary in order to advance medical knowledge. Some prominent voices of the time rejected even this notion, however. As Curnutt noted, "[S]uch noteworthy scholars as Alexander Pope [1688–1744] and Samuel Johnson [1709–1784] vehemently rejected vivisection as barbarous and cruel, as inclining its practitioners to mistreating people, and as advancing knowledge very little while failing to provide a cure for anything."[2]

Legislation has been passed to protect animals.

Protests such as this failed to make any changes until the rise of the animal welfare movement in England in the nineteenth century. In the United States, research animals would have to wait until 1966's Laboratory Animal Welfare Act (LAWA) before any major legislation would be passed in their favor. LAWA might not have passed at all were it not for an exposé published in the February 1966 issue of *Life* magazine that detailed the terrible conditions dogs were enduring at animal dealer facilities. Revised in 1970 as the Animal Welfare Act (AWA), this law now protects many "warm-blooded" animals being used in research, with the notable exception of birds and rodents.

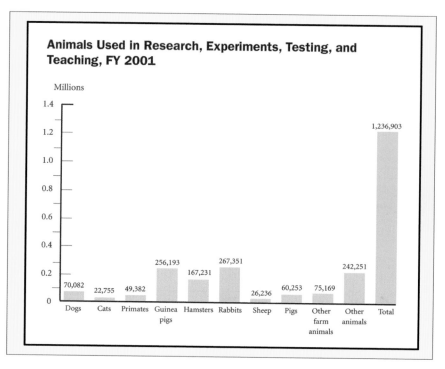

Animals Used in Research, Experiments, Testing, and Teaching, FY 2001

Because there has been so much controversy over the use of animal experimentation, the government is taking steps to better monitor the use of animals in scientific and industrial research. Facilities are now required to report how many animals they use in their tests (excluding birds and laboratory rats and mice, as well as certain farm animals used in agricultural research), and also whether the animals involved were subjected to pain and distress and under what conditions. These graphs contain the reported data from the fiscal year 2001.

Cruel and unnecessary tests should be banned.

Despite the passage of the AWA, many standard tests continue to be conducted that animal rights groups such as PETA believe seriously abuse animals. Two of the most infamous of these are the LD-50 and Draize tests.

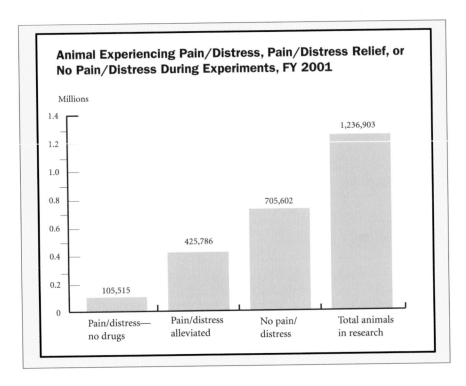

Animal Experiencing Pain/Distress, Pain/Distress Relief, or No Pain/Distress During Experiments, FY 2001

The LD-50 test was designed in 1927 by J. W. Trevan, a British pharmacologist, to discover the levels at which certain chemicals were lethal to animals. The name "LD-50" refers to the dosage level of a chemical that results in the deaths (LD = lethal dose) of 50 percent of the test subjects, usually rats. The rats that do not die from the test are later killed and studied, too. The dosage that resulted in half the rats' deaths is carefully recorded and becomes the accepted standard of what is considered an acutely toxic dose. Crystal Spiegel, outreach director for the American Anti-Vivisection Society, notes that the LD-50 test "is being phased out by other toxicological tests that are still lethal and harmful to animals, but use fewer individual animals."[3]

The Draize test was invented in the 1940s by John H. Draize, who at the time was a scientist for the U.S. Food and Drug Administration. This test was designed to measure the irritancy of cosmetics, cleaning products, and other commonly used house-hold goods. To check whether something was an irritant, a sample of the product is either put into a rabbit's eye (New Zealand white rabbits are usually used because they are very tame and easy to buy) or is applied to a patch of shaved skin that has been abraded. The rabbits, which are considered useful subjects because they lack tear ducts that may rinse the chemicals away, are restrained in a box or have their heads locked in stocks so they can't scratch at or rub their eyes or skin. Scientists then observe whether the test product causes the skin or eye to become inflamed. In the case of skin tests, the procedure is often used to see if a chemical is carcinogenic (causes cancer).

> • **How can one balance the importance of keeping human beings safe from faulty products against the fact that animals suffer pain or death in tests of products?**

When animal welfare activist Henry Spira decided to target cosmetics company Revlon in a campaign against the Draize test in 1978, he managed to convince the company to stop the practice. Slowly, other companies, such as Mary Kay Cosmetics, Proctor & Gamble, and Gillette, have also stopped using the Draize test. Other companies, however, such as the Dow Chemical Company, Johnson & Johnson, and Colgate-Palmolive, still use it, according to Curnutt.[4]

Animal rights groups have argued that the LD-50, Draize, and other tests were unnecessarily cruel, if they were even necessary at all. In fact, the Food and Drug Administration does not require that these tests be conducted to assure the safety of chemical products for humans, although the government does require testing of some sort. At least, one might argue, these experiments had a point, but as some activists have complained, many studies performed on animals seem to have no practical applications. A classic example involves Henry Spira again, who discovered in the late 1970s that the American Museum of Natural History was deliberately destroying parts of the brains of living cats, which would result in the cat's trying to mate with a rabbit. The cats were mutilated in other ways, too, such as having their sense of smell or sexual organs destroyed; the researchers would then record how this affected their sexual behavior. In Spira's view, these experiments were absurd and pointless, but they were still being funded by the U.S. government with grants of over $400,000. Through Spira's efforts, the funding was cut off and the experiments stopped.

Military Testing on Animals
(From PETA)

News programs have been airing ghastly video footage from Afghanistan that shows dogs dying agonizing deaths in al Qaeda military experiments. One tape shows a dog trapped in a room with vapor rising. The dog begins licking his chops (increased saliva is one of the first signs of poisoning), loses control of his hindquarters, and is eventually seen lying on his back, moaning. However, these cruel experiments are nothing new—nor are they confined to Afghanistan. The war on animals is an international one.

From Tel Aviv to Tehran to Texas, dogs and other animals are being poisoned and otherwise tortured in chemical, biological, and conventional warfare experiments. PETA has equally barbaric, secretly shot footage, from 1977, of Israeli soldiers injecting—and killing—dogs with what appear to be nerve agents.

No matter where you stand on international conflicts, it is a painful fact that the Israeli army has also blown up anaesthetized pigs with Scud missile explosives and conducted other painful experiments on dogs, monkeys, doves, mice, toads, and guinea pigs. An article in the March 17, 2000, issue of *Ha'aretz*, Israel's most respected daily newspaper, reported that experiments carried out by the Israel Defense Forces on animals were so horrific that the soldiers forced to conduct the experiments had to seek psychological counseling.

The United States military has a long history of conducting cruel animal experiments.

Uncounted Casualties

Each year, at least 320,000 primates, dogs, pigs, goats, sheep, rabbits, cats, and

[CONTINUED FROM PAGE 57]

other animals are hurt and killed by the U.S. Department of Defense (DoD) in experiments that rank among the most painful conducted in this country. Because these figures don't include experiments that were contracted out to non-governmental laboratories or the many sheep, goats, and pigs often shot in wound experiments, the total number of animal victims is actually much higher. The cost to taxpayers for these military experiments is estimated to be in excess of $100 million annually.

Top Secret

Military testing is classified "Top Secret," and it is very hard to get information about it. From published research, we do know that armed forces facilities all over the United States test all manner of weaponry on animals, from Soviet AK-47 rifles to biological and chemical warfare agents to nuclear blasts. Military experiments can be acutely painful, repetitive, costly, and unreliable, and they are particularly wasteful because most of the effects they study can be, or have already been, observed in humans or because the results cannot be extrapolated to human experience.

Sample Experiments

Burns and Blasts: As far back as in 1946, near the Bikini Atoll in the South Pacific, 4,000 sheep, goats, and other animals loaded onto a boat and set adrift were killed or severely burned by an atomic blast detonated above them. The military nicknamed the experiment "The Atomic Ark."

At the Army's Fort Sam Houston, live rats were immersed in boiling water for 10 seconds, and a group of them were infected on parts of their burned bodies. In 1987, at the Naval Medical Institute in Maryland, rats' backs were shaved, covered with ethanol, and then "flamed" for 10 seconds.

In 1988, at Kirtland Air Force Base in New Mexico, sheep were placed in a loose net sling against a reflecting plate, and an explosive device was detonated 19 meters away. In two of the experiments, 48 sheep were blasted: the first group to test the value of a vest worn during the blast, and the second to see if chemical markers would aid in the diagnosis of blast injury (they did not).

Radiation: At the Armed Forces Radiobiology Research Institute in Maryland, nine rhesus monkeys were strapped in chairs and exposed to total-body irradiation. Within two hours, six of the nine were vomiting, hypersalivating, and chewing. In another experiment, 17 beagles were exposed to total-body irradiation, studied for one to seven days, and then killed. The experimenter concluded that radiation affects the gall bladder.

At Brooks Air Force Base in Texas, rhesus monkeys were strapped to a B-52 flight simulator (the "Primate Equilibrium Platform"). After being prodded with painful electric shocks to learn to "fly" the device, the monkeys were irradiated with gamma rays to see if they could hold out for "the 10 hours it would take to bomb an imaginary Moscow." Those hit with the heaviest doses vomited violently and became extremely lethargic before being killed.

Diseases: To evaluate the effect of temperature on the transmission of the Dengue 2 virus, a mosquito-transmitted disease that causes fever, muscle pain, and rash, experiments conducted by the U.S. Army at Fort Detrich, Maryland, involved shaving the stomachs of adult rhesus monkeys and then attaching cartons of mosquitoes to their bodies to allow the mosquitoes to feed.

Experimenters at Fort Detrich have also invented a rabbit restraining device that consists of a small cage that pins the rabbits down with steel rods while mosquitoes feast on their bodies.

Wound Labs: The Department of Defense has operated "wound labs" since 1957. At these sites, conscious or semiconscious animals are suspended from slings and shot with high-powered weapons to inflict battle-like injuries for military surgical practice. In 1983, in response to public pressure, Congress limited the use of dogs in these labs, but countless goats, pigs, and sheep are still being shot, and at least one laboratory continues to shoot cats. At the Army's Fort Sam Houston "Goat Lab," goats are hung upside down and shot in their hind legs. After physicians practice excising the wounds, any goat who survives is killed.

In 1992 and again in 1994, doctors with the Physicians Committee for Responsible Medicine testified before Congress on military animal use and worked with the General Accounting Office in an investigation of Michael Carey's experiments at Louisiana State University. Carey shot 700 restrained cats in the head to "model" human injuries. As a result of the investigation, Carey's cat-shooting experiments were halted.

Other forms of military experiments include subjecting animals to decompression sickness, weightlessness, drugs and alcohol, smoke inhalation, and pure oxygen inhalation.

Source: "The Military's War on Animals." Available online at *http://www.peta.org/feat/military/*.

But such successes have been a mere drop in the bucket. Today, there are many ongoing research projects that animal rights groups maintain are completely unnecessary. A massive project started under the Clinton administration and spear-headed by then–Vice President Al Gore—and continuing today—is the Environmental Protection Agency's High Production Volume Chemical-Testing Program (HPV). The program was designed to test about 2,800 different chemicals commonly used in industries to see how environmentally safe they are. According to PETA, about one million animals will lose their lives in HPV tests to be conducted over a five-year period. Animals will be injected or fed chemicals, or will have chemicals rubbed into their eyes or on their skin, to check their reactions. Many of these chemicals are already known to be toxic, but because they haven't been run through the specific tests required by the HPV program, they will be tested again, even if animal research had been used in the past to determine toxicity. As PETA explains,

> Many animal tests performed in the past were conducted following slightly different methods than those currently required, which could mean that old test results will not be accepted under the HPV program. In addition, chemical com-panies are unlikely to submit data from previously conducted animal tests that show their chemicals to be harmful. It is more likely that companies will conduct new tests with the hope that the results will be more positive this time around.[5]

Another large-scale testing program that is similar to the HPV program but even greater in scope is the Endocrine Disruptor Screening Program (EDSP), which tests industrial chemicals for the specific purpose of seeing how they affect human hormones. When it is concluded, the EDSP will have tested between 5,000 and 87,000 chemicals on literally millions of lab animals.

Animal rights advocates protest against lab experiments not only because they find the tests cruel, but because they assert that the experiments are unnecessary or cause undue pain. Often, too, experiments that have already been conducted before are repeated, as the HPV program demonstrates.

The Silver Spring Monkeys case exposes laboratory conditions.

Laboratory conditions are another big concern for animal rights groups. While many researchers keep clean labs and properly feed their animals in accordance with the Animal Welfare Act, this has not always been the case. An infamous example of researcher abuse of animals has come to be known as the Silver Spring Monkey Case. PETA cofounder Alex Pacheco, who in 1981 was studying political science and environmental studies at George Washington University, decided to gain some laboratory experience by volunteering at the Institute for Behavioral Research in Silver Spring, Maryland. Here, various monkey species were having their limbs deliberately injured by scientists in order to discover new therapies for rehabilitating them that might eventually be applied to human beings. What Pacheco discovered in the labs, however, was shocking:

> The smell was incredible, intensifying as we entered the colony room where the monkeys were kept. I was astonished as I began to comprehend the conditions before me. I saw filth caked on the wires of the cages, feces piled in the bottom of the cages, urine and rust encrusting every surface. There, amid this rotting stench, sat sixteen crab-eating macaques and one rhesus monkey, their lives limited to metal boxes just 17¾ inches wide. In their desperation to assuage their hunger, they were picking forlornly at scraps and fragments of broken biscuits that had fallen through the wire into the sodden

accumulations in the waste collection trays below. The cages had clearly not been cleaned properly for months. There were no dishes to keep the food away from the feces, nothing for the animals to sit on but the jagged wires of the old cages, nothing for them to see but the filthy, feces-splattered walls of that windowless room, only 15 ft. square.[6]

Pacheco further noted that medicines and sacks of food used in the lab had all expired years before—sometimes more than ten years before. He also observed the bizarre behavior of the animals and that they had not received proper medical treatment; sometimes, clearly visible injuries had not been bandaged. To add insult to injury, the monkeys were being put under the care of people with little or no experience (Pacheco himself was put in charge of a project even though he was just a college student with no laboratory background whatsoever) and forced to endure apparently pointless and cruel experiments. For example, Pacheco was told to starve two of his monkey subjects and then taunt them with food, which he would not be allowed to give them. In another experiment, he was told to clamp a hemostat (a device normally used to compress a bleeding vessel) onto the testicles of a monkey and write down his observations as the monkey reacted to the pain. The entire purpose of such research, as far as he could gather from Dr. Edward Taub, the head of the lab, was not to discover something useful but simply to obtain grant money from the National Institutes of Health.

After gathering data on the lab's conditions and the treatment of the animals, as well as getting a number of witnesses to agree to help him, Pacheco took his case to the police. It eventually went to trial, and in 1981, Taub was found guilty of six counts of animal cruelty and denying his animals proper veterinary care.[7] Taub took the case to the

Maryland Court of Appeals, and although Maryland had laws against animal cruelty, because Taub was working under the auspices of a federal grant, the court decided that the laws did not apply to him and reversed the earlier court decision.[8] Despite the ultimate failure of the case, it helped gain national attention for the animal rights movement.

Are conditions in all laboratories as awful as they were at the Institute for Behavioral Research? Probably not, since the AWA does seem to have improved the situation. However, many animal rights activists assert that the improvements made so far are not enough. As Michael W. Fox notes in *Inhumane Society,* "Today's standards do not consider the animals' social, emotional, and environmental needs."[9]

> • **Some people have compared animal experimentation with the Holocaust. Using the Silver Spring Monkeys case as a model, how many parallels can one draw between these two events?**

Medical research on animals does not help science.

Not only are experiments on animals often painful and sometimes not even designed to find cures for human ailments, but even the studies directed at human applications are misguided, according to some animal rights activists. C. Ray Greek, a medical doctor, and Jean Swingle Greek, a veterinarian, are cofounders of Americans for Medical Advancement. In their book *Sacred Cows and Golden Geese: The Human Cost of Experiments on Animals,* they note that because animal and human biology are not the same, test results from nonhuman species are not applicable to human beings. Because a positive result in an animal might not produce the same effect in a human, "thousands of people get sick from legal pharmaceuticals" each year, they assert.[10] In addition, nonhuman animals make poor test subjects because they can't communicate effectively to researchers when they are experiencing pain or other negative side effects from an experiment. Thus, researchers only see an adverse result when an animal is in such excruciating pain that the symptoms become overt.

Even when animal testing is used, the next step in researching a drug is always human testing. The Greeks write, "When compounds demonstrate therapeutic effect on an animal, therapeutic effect without ill side effect, they proceed to human clinical trials. There, very often—our research shows anywhere from 52 to 100 percent of the time—they fail, frequently by wounding or killing people. Animal testing has made it look as if given compounds will not injure humans, but they do."[11] The Greeks provide several examples of drugs that were tested on animals but still produced acute negative effects on humans. Diethylstilbestrol, for one, was a drug that was supposed to prevent miscarriages in pregnant women, but it actually had the opposite effect; thalidomide, another drug used by pregnant women, caused birth defects; isoproterenol, a drug for treating asthma, was toxic to humans; etanerecept, used for patients with rheumatoid arthritis, caused infections and, in some cases, death; perhexiline, a medicine for treating heart disease, caused liver failure.

> • **Medical science is not an exact process. Mistakes are frequently made, just as serendipitous discoveries sometimes occur. How many risks should we take in order to produce a new medicine or treatment that may save human lives?**

Sacred Cows and Golden Geese also makes interesting observations about the other negative effects of the insistence on animal testing in drug research. For example, not only do drugs that were tested on animals and subsequently approved for human use sometimes cause problems, but the government also insists that drugs that appear to be effective on people later be tested on animals. If they prove to be harmful to other species, the drugs are withdrawn from the market, thus denying people medications that might have been helpful to them. That such logic can be fallacious is demonstrated by the example of acetaminophen, the painkiller used in over-the-counter drugs such as Tylenol. Millions of people use Tylenol regularly. However, if a cat is given a single dose, it will probably die of renal failure. The Greeks pursue this train of thought further by asking,

> Can we actually credit experimentation on animals as having prevented the FDA from releasing a medication that would have been dangerous to humans? This is difficult to assess, obviously, since such drugs never progressed to market. However, it is worth remarking that countries that do not rely on animal testing have no higher incidence of adverse-drug reactions than the United States, and frequently have access to the latest drugs years before we do. [12]

There are alternatives to animal tests.

Not very many years ago, before the creation of crash-test dummies, the automobile industry used live baboons to see how safe their cars were in simulated accidents. As one might imagine, putting a live primate in a car and hurling it toward a wall at fast speeds resulted in serious injuries or death for many baboons. Auto industry executives insisted that the tests were necessary, however, to ensure that cars were meeting government guidelines for consumer safety. When the public protested the use of animals, however, the crash-test dummy was invented as an alternative. Not only did the invention of these dummies prevent animals from being harmed, but researchers have actually found them to be more useful than baboons for recording accurate data.

Many animal liberationists assert that there are alternatives that can replace live test subjects for medical research. For example, with new advances in technology, mathematical models can be created on computers (called *in silico* testing). For example, a treatment for AIDS (acquired immuno-deficiency syndrome) using what are called protease inhibitors was developed largely through the use of computer models. Computers can't perfectly duplicate what happens in a real body, of course, but they are also not the only alternative.

Scientists use cell cultures in what is called *in vitro* testing, or tests performed in test tubes or other containers. The advantage here is that human cells can be used instead of animal cells to see how they react to chemicals that are being checked for toxicity or drugs being developed for medical treatments such as cancer. For example, the infamous Draize eye and skin tests can now be replaced with Irritection Assay, an *in vitro* test that not only eliminates the need for animals but can also produce results in about five hours, as opposed to about two to three weeks for *in vivo* (live animal) tests. It is also easier to reproduce results for verification with *in vitro* than *in vivo* testing, and research has shown that Irritection Assay is just as reliable as the Draize test.

Other tests available to researchers include the Ames Test, which uses the bacteria *Salmonella typhimurium* to check for chemical carcinogenicity (whether chemicals cause cancer) and mutagenicity (whether they cause muta-tions); the Hayes Test, which is similar to the Ames Test but uses *E. coli* bacteria instead; and the Limulus amebocyte lysate (LAL) test, which checks for endotoxins that may cause fevers.

Still another alternative is the use of "lower organisms," such as plants or invertebrates, or the use of animal embryos. Also, since most drug testing still requires human beings to be tested at some point, people could be used more often than they are now. This suggestion is not as inhumane as it might seem at first, since advances in technology have made it possible to perform tests on people noninvasively. Procedures such as magnetoencephalography, positron emission tomography, and nuclear magnetic resonance make it possible to perform many experiments without harming people. Also, human cell cultures can be grown in the lab; specialized human cells or fragments of cells can be used for very specialized tests that give accurate results for medical research, since they come from people and not animals.

Where is animal experimentation going?

With advances in genetics, animal testing in recent years is reaching levels once dreamed of only in science fiction. New procedures are being created that might make it possible, for example, to alter a pig's internal organs so that they resemble those of a human being. The organs might then be extracted from the pig and transplanted into a person in a process known as xenotransplantation. In another case of genetic alteration, researchers in South Dakota have created cows whose bodies are being programmed to produce antibodies that treat infections in human beings. If such research proves successful, we may someday see the establishment of animal farms whose purpose is not to produce meat or dairy products, but rather to grow human organs and medicines.

The boom in the new field of genetic research is having new and previously unimagined consequences for laboratory animals. As Crystal Spiegel of the American Anti-Vivisection Society notes:

> Cloning and genetic research has resulted in a *drastic* increase in the numbers of animals in laboratories, especially mice, rats, and birds. Most of these animals are killed (as laboratory "waste") because they do not exhibit desired traits. Animals who have been genetically manipulated suffer in unknown ways, as they are unique

creatures. I have heard veterinarians at scientific confer-
ences state that they do not know how to properly care
for them because the death rates are high and you never
know when their bodies will "malfunction." Furthermore, researchers try to manipulate nonhuman animals
to carry human-specific diseases and other maladies. But
these are not the same as natural occurrences, especially
in another species altogether.[13]

Even without genetic research, current methods in
traditional animal research are difficult to eliminate because
of the status quo. Peter Singer concludes that animal experimentation continues for a number of reasons. First, he says,
speciesism in the scientific community is still common.
People still don't see animals and their suffering as being
as important as human needs. Second, experiments with
animals continue because researchers are familiar with them
and to change how they do their work would require a
special effort. As Singer writes:

> Once a pattern of animal experimentation becomes
> the accepted mode of research in a particular field, the
> process is self-reinforcing and difficult to break out of.
> Not only publications and promotions but also the
> awards and grants that finance research become geared
> to animal experiments. A proposal for a new experiment
> with animals is something that the administrators of
> research funds will be ready to support, if they have in
> the past supported other experiments on animals. New
> nonanimal-using methods will seem less familiar and will
> be less likely to receive support.[14]

Another reason for the continuation of *in vivo* testing is
simply the government bureaucracy. *In vitro* and other alternative testing methods have not yet been well established, and

approval from the U.S. Food and Drug Administration takes a long time. As Jordan Curnutt commented, "Given the decades-long emphasis on *in vivo* . . . testing found in federal regulations, the development of alternatives has been stymied: regulated industries and progressive biotech companies must face laboring to develop *in vitro* and other options without an established method for gaining governmental acceptance." [15]

- **Animal rights advocates often say that an ounce of prevention is worth a pound of cure. Should the government and universities put more work and money into emphasizing preventive measures to disease, and, if they did, might this eliminate the need for animal testing?**

Animal rights supporters believe that animal research is inherently cruel and should be replaced with other available forms of testing. They argue that animals are generally too physically different from human beings for the results of animal testing to be accurate anyway.

Animals Serve a Useful Purpose in Medical Research

For thousands of years, humanity was plagued by an insidious virus that infected people's nervous systems. It often caused paralysis and even death. The disease was terrifying, feeding on human civilization until the 1950s. Because it was easily spread in community settings and children were particularly vulnerable, parents often forbade their children to swim in public pools for fear of acquiring this virus. But adults could contract it as well, including, most famously, President Franklin D. Roosevelt, who was confined to a wheelchair because of his illness, though he tried as much as possible to hide his handicap from the public. The disease is known as paralytic poliomyelitis—or polio, for short. Before a cure was found, many stricken children had to use crutches and leg braces to walk, and hospital wards were full of patients who had to live out their lives confined to a bed inside iron lungs that allowed them to breathe. Tens of thousands of Americans were affected every year.

It was President Roosevelt who declared a war on polio, and with the government funding he helped provide, Dr. Jonas Salk discovered a vaccine in 1955. Thanks to his work, polio, which was once rampant all over the world, has now been eliminated in all but the poorest nations. How did Salk discover his amazing vaccine? Through animal research. Dr. Alfred Sabin, who also worked on the cure for polio, later commented, "My own experience of more than 60 years in biomedical research amply demonstrate that without the use of animals and human beings, it would have been impossible to acquire the important knowledge needed to prevent much suffering and premature death not only amongst humans but also amongst animals." [1]

There are many other benefits to medical research with animals.

Polio is not the only disease that was eliminated or significantly reduced with the help of animal research, however. The extensive list includes measles, smallpox (which has now been eradicated), influenza (the flu), anthrax, tuberculosis, rabies, whooping cough, infectious hepatitis, and diphtheria. Many advances in treatments for diabetes (such as the use of insulin), arthritis, tuberculosis, infertility, several forms of cancer, heart disease, and AIDS, among other diseases, have been created thanks to animal research. Modern-day surgical procedures such as organ repairs and transplants, artificial knees, spinal cord repair, and genetic and stem cell research are also the result of animal experimentation.

- **Many cures for diseases have been discovered through animal research. What do you think the world would be like today if these discoveries hadn't been made? Would it have been worth saving the lives of the animals that died in the research process?**

Prominent physicians have repeatedly upheld the necessity of animal research in the area of medicine. For example, former U.S. Surgeon General Everett Koop has asserted, "We would be in absolute, utter darkness about AIDS if we hadn't done decades of basic research in animals . . . before we even knew there was AIDS."[2] Nobel Prize–winner Sir John Vane further notes, "The medicines of tomorrow will depend upon research being done today, for which animal experimentation is essential. Ignore the need for that research and we shall lose the cures that we are entitled to expect in the next 50 years for illnesses that afflict hundreds of millions of people such as cancer, heart disease, viral diseases, malaria, schistosomiasis and sickle cell anaemia."[3] The world medical community has repeatedly acknowledged the value of animal research by awarding about two-thirds of the Nobel Prizes in physiology or medicine to researchers who made medical advances through the use of animal experimentation. In a survey of 39 Nobel laureates who received the prize in physiology or medicine, 97 percent agreed with the statement that animal research has been vital for the advancement of medicine in the past; 92 percent further agreed that it still remains essential today.[4]

Medical Advances Due to Animal Research

- Antibiotics for the treatment of bacterial infections
- Vaccines for smallpox, tetanus, diphtheria, polio, measles, lyme disease, hepatitis B and chicken pox, gene therapy, insulin to control diabetes
- Anticoagulants, anesthesia, and neuromuscular blocking agents
- Chemotherapy for cancer patients
- Pacemaker implants to treat cardiac patients
- Discovery of the HIV virus and development of drugs to control the progression of AIDS
- Organ transplantation techniques

Source: Americans for Medical Progress

As Frankie Trull, president of the Foundation for Biomedical Research, asserts, without animal research "we probably wouldn't have [the possibility of] cures for Alzheimer's disease, paralysis (spinal cord injuries), diabetes, cystic fibrosis. A lot of diseases that are still very prevalent in this society: certain types of cancer, heart disease, most anything you can think of we probably wouldn't have cures ever, or certainly during the next two lifetimes." [5]

Animals are similar enough to humans to make them useful in experiments.

One argument that animal rights groups make against animal research is that dogs, cats, monkeys, rats, mice, and other animals are different species and, therefore, what works for them will not necessarily work for a human being. But while the differences between the species are obvious to anyone, medical researchers will say that they target the similarities in their studies. With advances in genetic engineering, animals that carry human genes can be bred in laboratories and then be used to produce results similar to what they would be in human beings. According to a pro–animal research group known as the Incurably Ill for Animal Research:

> There are over 250 diseases that are common to both humans and animals. Many treatments are also the same in both veterinary and human medicine. Diabetes occurs in cats, dogs, monkeys and humans, and they all use insulin to control their blood sugar levels. The same heart pacemakers that save human lives also have saved many pet dogs. The polio vaccine we use to protect our children is also given to chimpanzees in the wild to control outbreaks of polio.
>
> Scientists carefully choose animal models that are properly suited to the condition being studied. For instance, dogs were used in the development of pacemakers, bypass surgery and balloon angioplasty (widening narrow arteries) because their cardiovascular system is very similar to humans. Laboratory mice may now be genetically engineered with human

characteristics. One strain actually has an immune system that is identical to that of a human, offering researchers a great model for studying various types of cancer and AIDS. When it comes to disease processes, man and animals have many similarities.[6]

Michael Allen Fox similarly asserts in *The Case for Animal Experimentation* that there are many physiological and behavioral similarities between animals and humans. If one accepts the theory of evolution, that all animals descended from similar ancestors millions of years ago, then it stands to reason that many of our basic biological traits are shared. Fox uses the example of hemoglobin in our red blood cells, which carry oxygen through our bodies. Fox comments that "though there are many different hemoglobins in nature, the chimpanzee's is identical to our own,"[7] and researchers have shown that the proteins in our bodies are 99 percent identical to those in chimps. These similarities don't just apply to other primates, such as chimps, though. As Fox continues, "Some animals as far removed from humans as mice, hamsters, and guinea pigs exhibit very similar physiological reactions; dogs share many of the same diseases; and pigs have been noted to be strikingly like humans physiologically and anatomically."[8]

Besides the applications for drug and surgical procedure development, animals are also used in behavioral research. Though the benefits of this type of research might not be as evident as research that produces drugs or surgical therapies, many psychologists and psychiatrists attest to its importance. "Such lab research provides a scientific foundation for a variety of behavioral treatments—psychotherapy, assertiveness training, meditation, and relaxation training with or without biofeedback," according to experimental psychologist Neal Miller.[9] Animals can be used in such research because many species—and this is where higher primates such as chimps and gorillas have proven especially useful—display attitudes, social relationships, and other behaviors that are remarkably similar to those of humans.

- **If the same animal research that benefits a human being also benefits other animal species, wouldn't this help to justify such experiments? Why or why not?**

Because the benefits of doing research in which scientists deliberately try to alter the behavior of animals is not always readily apparent, psychological studies on animals is perhaps even more controversial than medical research. Still, many proponents assert that it is very important in finding treatments for people who suffer from addictions and other behavioral problems. "It gets really tricky," admits Frankie Trull. But, she adds:

> I think that people who have addictive problems, alcoholism, whatever, psychiatric problems, still have a major issue in our society, meaning we view these problems as human weaknesses. Science doesn't see it that way. First of all, the suffering that these people go through is huge, the cost to society is huge, and if research has to be done in behavioral areas then it's still going to be done in animal models. I think it's much trickier to explain . . . but that doesn't minimize the disease. And they are diseases. Mental illness is a disease just like cancer. [With animal research] that's where they're doing a lot of neurological studies where they're studying the brain. They train animals to have behavioral responses to certain things. It's tricky, but that's the old rat through the maze.[10]

Animals are needed for research duplication.

Another allegation that animal rights supporters make is that researchers unnecessarily repeat experiments on animals just to get more grant money. Research scientists respond to this accusation in several ways. First of all, results from a single experiment are not sufficient proof that the data obtained are valid. In order to be sure that the conclusions drawn are correct, accepted scientific method dictates that experiments must be repeated and the results duplicated. If the same results are duplicated by other researchers, then it is generally agreed that no errors were made in the original experiment. This is important so that, for example, a drug is not created based on the results of a test that might be erroneous, the consequences of which could be dangerous, if not lethal. "It is important to add," according to the Incurably Ill for Animal Research, "that while it may appear to a casual observer that one experiment is like another, we must be very careful about such observations. Small but very important differences in chemistry, for example, may be the difference between life and death."[11]

> • **How extensively should a drug be tested before it goes to market? Can a drug ever be tested enough to ensure that it is 100 percent safe and effective? How long should disease sufferers be expected to wait for a new drug that might save their lives?**

As for the accusation that researchers repeat experiments as part of their quest for grant money, the Incurably Ill for Animal Research responds:

> There is far less money available to fund research projects than there are grant applications for that money. Therefore, competition eliminates marginal experiments as a matter of course. For example, the National Institutes of Health, which funds most biomedical research (about 90% of basic research and 2/3 of clinical research), has experts in every field to review grant applications and recommend those worthy of funding. Of the applications recommended for funding, they have money for only about 25%. Reviewers are extremely careful to assure they fund only those applicants who propose to explore the frontiers of science, not those who propose to repeat history.[12]

The belief that money is a main motivating factor for people conducting animal research is not reflective of reality, say research advocates. As the numbers above indicate, funding from government resources is hard to come by, and there aren't any scientists becoming fabulously wealthy from their grants alone. Medical research scientists, for example, receive much less pay than physicians who work in hospitals or private practice caring for patients. As for the large pharmaceutical companies that develop drugs for people, they can spend millions of dollars and years of research just to create a single drug.

Some opponents of animal experimentation assert that if more money were spent on preventive medicine—such as campaigns to encourage people to follow a healthier lifestyle and, therefore, get sick less often—then we would be able to significantly reduce or eliminate animal research entirely. Such an argument, says Trull, is not realistic:

> I think that it is an incredibly simplistic argument. I've often heard the animal rights people say, "If we didn't drink alcohol, smoke cigarettes, or eat red meat there would be no disease and therefore we wouldn't have to do animal research." Would that life were that simple. Of course prevention is important, and that's a personal responsibility that people should take on, you know, the big issue; the big public issue that everyone is talking about is obesity, and it is a legitimate concern. That, for some people, is completely self-driven, and for other people it's genetic. There are a lot of things that need to be learned about obesity, and they're studying that now in obese genetic animals. But animal research for the foreseeable future is still pivotal.[13]

Conditions in laboratories are not as bad as they are depicted as being.

Much publicity in the campaign against animal research has been devoted to the living conditions of animals in laboratories—as evidenced in the Silver Spring Monkeys case. Research advocates, however, maintain that such examples of animal abuse are rare and, with all the government legislation that is now in place, unlikely to be repeated very often in the scientific community.

The Animal Welfare Act (AWA) regulates conditions in research facilities that use animals; any lab that receives federal government funding or that receives animals from another state is subject to the AWA. As part of this, labs have to be licensed by the Food and Drug Administration (FDA) and are subjected to inspections—often unannounced—by the Animal and Plant Health Inspection Service (APHIS). Laboratories have to report the number and species of animals in their facilities; they have to work with APHIS-licensed animal dealers; their animals have to be checked by veterinarians on a regular basis; and researchers and technicians have to be fully trained and qualified.

> • **How many laws are necessary to protect the lives and safety of animals? Should all these laws be compiled under the Animal Welfare Act, or is it all right that some guidelines are covered under other laws and regulations?**

In addition, the National Institutes of Health (NIH) has published the *Guide for the Care and Use of Laboratory Animals,* which delineates standards for animal care—including rodents and birds—for all federally funded laboratories in the United States. Under the NIH guidelines, all labs must set up committees that are responsible for overseeing animal care. The committee must include a veterinarian and at least one person who is not an employee at the research facility. Any violations of federal or NIH guidelines that the committee members observe must be reported to the NIH. This kind of oversight, say those who support continued animal research, assures that lab animals are provided with humane treatment. Trull adds:

> There are a lot of reasons to care for laboratory animals. Obviously, there is the moral reason to care and the ethical reasons to care, but also animals that are stressed provide unreliable research results, so it's a waste of everybody's time if you can't keep this animal comfortable. The regulations that govern the labs themselves are more restrictive than the regulations that

govern human research. All research facilities operate under what's called the Animal Welfare Act, which has standards for the facilities themselves, like the HVAC systems and how many air exchanges there have to be per minute. It gets actually quite sophisticated and quite complicated, and it's very expensive.[14]

> • **Do you believe that animal researchers intentionally harm or abuse the animals in their laboratories? Is it possible that animal rights groups focus only on a small minority of wrongheaded researchers to make their case, or do you think deliberate animal abuse is common?**

Proponents of animal testing also assert that animal rights groups overemphasize the use of animals such as cats, dogs, rabbits, and monkeys, which have much more sympathetic appeal to most people. In fact, dogs and cats make up only about one percent of the animals used yearly in laboratories, whereas 90 percent are rats or mice, with the remaining 9 percent being primates and other species. Rats, mice, and birds are not covered under the AWA, as specified in a regulatory definition issued by the APHIS in 1972. This regulation was challenged by the Humane Society of the United States (HSUS) and the Animal Legal Defense Fund (ALDF), which filed a lawsuit in the District of Columbia Circuit Court against Mike Espy, who at that time was the U.S. secretary of agriculture.[15] The court ruled against the ALDF in this case. Nevertheless, this doesn't mean that rodents and birds go unprotected. As Trull states:

> The vast majority of rodents and birds are covered under other things, like anybody who receives NIH funding—which is almost all if not all of the academic institutions in the country, so all the medical schools, the veterinary schools, the teaching hospitals—they have to comply with the NIH *Guide for the Care and Use of Laboratory Animals*. Companies that are trying to get products approved through the Food and Drug Administration

have to comply with the Good Laboratory Practices Act. So a lot of these animals are covered in duplicative ways, but the vast majority are covered by one set of regulations or another.[16]

For some research, there are no good alternatives to animal experimentation.

Although new methods are becoming available to scientists, animal testing advocates say that none of these alternatives can fully replace the use of animals. This is because the newer tests are done in isolation outside of a living body and, therefore, can't indicate whether other unforeseen reactions might take place. The physiology of any living organism is much more complex than what can be duplicated in a test tube or Petri dish because animals have numerous biological systems, including the immune system, nervous system, and endocrine system, that interact with one another. An *in vitro* test designed to examine the reaction of skin tissue to a chemical, for example, might not foresee a reaction within the nervous system of a living organism. Similarly, computer modeling, while useful to a certain extent, necessarily simplifies what actually occurs in organic systems. Thus far, these alternative tests have not been successful in proving whether or not a certain chemical will cause birth defects or cancer.

Researchers are glad to use these alternatives to animal testing whenever possible, but they generally recognize that such methods will never completely replace animals in the lab. Instead, the accepted response to demands for the elimination of animal experimentation is what has become known as "the Three R's": *replacement, reduction,* and *refinement.* First proposed back in 1957 by W.M.S. Russell in his book *The Increase of Humanity in Experimentation,* the Three R's are guidelines for cutting back the use of animals as much as feasible without sacrificing the accuracy of tests. The first R, *replacement,* obviously refers to using other testing methods, like those described above.

Reduction, the second R, refers to cutting back on unnecessary waste. Reduction can be accomplished by using the same animals more than once. For example, if a researcher is about to perform an *in vivo* procedure on the heart of an animal that will cause it to die, he or she can inform colleagues beforehand so that if another scientist was planning to perform an experiment on another organ, such as a liver or kidney, the same animal could be used. The British organization Fund for the Replacement of Animals in Medical Experiments (FRAME) further recommends that "appropriate experimental design and appropriate analysis of the resulting data . . . can increase the precision of the data and at the same time enable fewer animals to be used for the generation of these data." [17] FRAME goes on to suggest that better upfront planning can reduce waste. For instance, "a small pilot study will indicate whether or not it is appropriate to proceed to a major experiment."

Finally, the third R, *refinement*, refers to improving animals' living conditions throughout their time in the lab, including providing them with more interesting surroundings (tubes for mice to hide in, toys for dogs and cats) and interaction with others of their own species or with people. This is not only kinder to the animals but also results in better science, as FRAME points out: "The experience of pain and other stress is likely to result in physiological changes which may increase the variability of experimental results." [18] This same logic applies when the time comes to actually use an animal in a medical procedure. Whenever possible, researchers use anesthetics or analgesics (painkillers that do not cause the patient to lose consciousness) to minimize pain in their test subjects. The use of painkillers is mandated by the AWA and the NIH, except in those cases where it is necessary to withhold medication, such as when a researcher is working to develop new medicines to reduce pain or studying the effects of pain on behavior.

- **Is it enough for researchers to follow the "Three R's" in reducing potential harm on animals in experiments, or would it be better to make a clean, abrupt break from animal research and hope that alternatives will be enough to replace live animals?**

Other uses of animal experimentation may be necessary.

Whereas the above discussion has focused on the use of animals for medical tests, animal subjects are also used in the testing of products such as cosmetics (the focus of many animal liberationists who protest things such as the Draize test) and household cleaners. Although it certainly can't be argued that a new brand of oven cleaner is as important as a breakthrough drug that will treat a deadly disease, new chemicals are nonetheless being marketed every year for use in industry and households and all of them must be tested for their safety, as mandated by government regulations set down by the Food and Drug Administration, the Environmental Protection Agency, and the Consumer Product Safety Commission. The High Production Volume Chemical-Testing Program, in which thousands of chemicals are being retested for safety, is protested by animal rights groups because, for one thing, many chemicals that are known to be toxic (such as turpentine and arsenic) are being tested again on animals. However, the point of these tests is not always to show that certain chemicals are dangerous, but rather to show *how* dangerous they are. Inevitably, many of these products are going to leak out into the environment. The point of the HPV program is to determine at what levels they will become a major threat to human safety.

Another area not often addressed by animal rights groups, according to those in favor of research, is that animal experimentation has also been highly beneficial to veterinary medicine. Without such research, treatments for common and serious diseases, including feline leukemia, parvovirus, rabies, and distemper, could not have been created; nor would medicines that treat parasites such as ticks, fleas, heartworms, and hookworms, which can be lethal to dogs and cats, have been developed. Animals used in agriculture also benefit greatly from veterinary research. Since the animals used in research in these cases are the same species as those the tests are intended to benefit, it is particularly germane to this field of study. In addition, many medicines originally developed for people have been found to help animals as well.

Scientists fear that the progress that they have made through the use of animal research will come to an end if anti-vivisectionists and other animal rights groups have their way. As Robert J. White concludes in an article for the *American Scholar:*

> At the urging of a small but determined group of antivivisec-tionists, the United States Congress is constantly considering legislation that, if enacted into law, will seriously restrict the freedom of individual scientists participating in medical research, in the same way that laws have so seriously hampered similar research in Britain. . . . Unless American medicine and its allied biological professions cast off their mantles of detachment and undertake the responsibility of educating through established lines of communication our citizens to the necessities of medical research, the antivivisection movement may eventually win the day.[19]

Those who support animal research argue that past results, such as the near-eradication of polio, demonstrate conclusively that animal testing is highly accurate. They also believe that, in situations where tests would be too dangerous for human subjects, animals are the only reasonable alternative.

Animals Should Not Be Used for Food and Clothing

Although the use of animals in medical experimentation has certainly received a great deal of press, the number of animals exploited for food and clothing is many times greater than the number used in research. Animal rights groups often use lab experiments to illustrate animal abuse because the idea of surgery and chemical tests creates vivid pictures of animals in torment. Also, getting people to protest medical testing is perhaps less difficult than getting them to give up eating meat or drinking milk. People seeking more liberties for animals, however, also strenuously emphasize what they see as the evils of using animals in agriculture, of harvesting animals for their fur and hides, and of hunting them with guns and traps. People's habits of eating meat and wearing fur are not only exploitive of animals, say rights advocates, but they are bad for our health and for the environment.

Modern farms are more like factories.

Because the U.S. population has become so urbanized in recent decades, the majority of Americans are unaware of what life on a modern farm is really like these days. We often picture a farm as a pleasant house in the countryside with a barn for the animals and a farmyard that provides plenty of space and sunshine for them to enjoy. The farmer walks out in his overalls and spreads feed out for his chickens and dumps slop into a big trough for his pigs.

Today, however, the reality is very different. Because of economic changes and the continued growth of human populations, the majority of animals are now raised on a few very large farms rather than on many small, traditional farms. Pigs, chickens, and sometimes cattle are confined by the thousands and even tens of thousands in one building that allows very little freedom for movement. Many of these buildings are remarkably high-tech. Automated methods have been developed to feed and clean up after the animals, which can spend their entire lives indoors without ever having a chance to see a barnyard.

To keep them healthy and make them grow large and fat in these cramped conditions, animals are given hormones and antibiotics, which pro–animal rights people say are then passed along to humans when we eat hamburgers, steaks, pork chops, and chicken nuggets made from these meats. Also, because there is such a rush to get animals out to the slaughterhouse, cattle, pigs, and chickens are at times shipped out to market even before they reach full maturity. Administering hormones and force-feeding, for example, make broiler chickens (those destined for the slaughterhouse) large enough for shipping when they are only seven to eight weeks old. Furthermore, chickens are made to lay eggs at an extraordinary rate, and cows, especially those in the dairy industry, are made to give birth over and over until they are so physically exhausted that their lifespan is shortened considerably, according to activists who protest such conditions.

> • **Factory farms are designed to produce the most meat, eggs, and dairy products as efficiently as possible. How much more would you be willing to pay at the grocery store to end factory farms and current slaughterhouse methods and return to agricultural methods that resemble early twentieth-century practices?**

C. David Coats, writing in *Old MacDonald's Factory Farm,* comments that sows (female pigs) can be made to produce 100 to 110 piglets in about four or five years, after which they are so exhausted that they are no longer of any use for bearing young. At that point, the sows are shipped to the slaughter-house. Coats continues:

> To be efficient as a reproductive unit, the sow must produce the maximum number of live piglets in the shortest time. By force-weaning piglets at an unnaturally early age, operators can reimpregnate the sow sooner and accelerate the normal reproductive cycle. No regard is paid for the distress and suffering caused by these continual pregnancies, separations, and frustrated maternal instincts.[1]

Sows are placed in a gestation crate, where they are sometimes chained as well, that measures about two feet wide by six feet long. This provides no room for movement and forces the pig to eat, sleep, urinate, and defecate all in the same place. Under such conditions, the animals develop stereotypical behaviors, such as swaying and bar chewing. "According to research in Holland," says Coats, "these repetitive movements, or stereotypes, are 'coping behaviors'—indicators of psychological disturbance instinctively developed to deal with the stress of understimulation and confinement."[2] Pigs that become neurotic because of their close quarters will sometimes chew on each others' tails. To prevent this, the solution at factory farms has been to cut off their tails.

Similar treatment is given to cows and chickens. Cows are confined to barns or in pens, where they spend their entire lives.

The fate for dairy cows is in some ways even more drastic than for an animal raised for meat. As Andrew Butler of PETA explains:

> Most people surprisingly don't even realize that cows have to be pregnant in order to produce milk just like all other mammals. They don't just mysteriously and magically produce milk. They suffer through a constant cycle of impregnation and birth; cows that would normally live for 25 years or more are worn out after this constant cycle after just five short years. When their milk production drops, they are kicked and prodded down the slaughter ramp just like all the other animals and go through that whole hideous process.
>
> Also, just like all other animals, cows give milk for their babies, and they aren't allowed to nurse their own young. Instead, in the case of male calves . . . those calves are allowed to nurse for a day, often no longer than that. Then they're shipped off to the veal crate, where they'll spend 17 weeks in intensive confinement, unable to turn around, to lie down, or exercise in any way in order to keep their muscles weak. They're fed a diet of gruel other than their mother's milk in order to keep them anemic, and then of course they're slaughtered for veal. And most people also don't know that those industries are so closely linked—that the veal industry, which is very widely regarded as a cruel one, is part and parcel of the whole dairy industry.[3]

The fate of veal calves has been more publicized than other forms of meat, and, consequently, many Americans have refused to eat veal. On the other hand, annual consumption of poultry in the United States has skyrocketed from 40.3 pounds per person in 1970 to 75.6 pound per person in 2001. Chicken factory farms have grown accordingly.

On these farms, chickens are placed in such tight quarters—in buildings holding anywhere between 10,000 and 100,000 birds—that they sometimes become aggressive with each other. So that the birds will not hurt themselves in fights, they endure a process called "debeaking," in which part of each chicken's beak is cut off. In what animal rights people feel is another egregious abuse, hens that will be used to lay eggs are artificially stimulated through the use of lighting to begin laying before they have fully matured. Sometimes, the result, as Michael W. Fox reports in *Eating with a Conscience,* is what those in the industry call blowout—"the hens' vents (posteriors) burst, and they die."[4]

> • **With most Americans living in the city or in suburbs, how much do you think people are aware of what is occurring today on farms? Do you believe that people are apathetic about farm life since most have never experienced it firsthand?**

There are many health concerns caused by the use of animals.

There are many health concerns regarding animal farming, say those who oppose it, both for animals and for people. Because hundreds or thousands of animals live inside a single building, gases and particles emitted by excrement are easily carried through the air, making diseases such as respiratory ailments a common concern. Fox adds, "Once farmers push animals' productivity too far, disease incidence increases. Effects of over-feeding high-energy 'concentrates' to dairy cows and beef cattle contribute significantly to a variety of health problems. These include fatty liver disease, mastitis, crippling foot diseases, and overall weakening of the immune system, which results in higher incidence of infectious diseases."[5] Commenting on the health issues for both people and animals, Butler asserts that:

A lot of meat is full of hormones and antibiotics because animals are given growth hormones in order to maximize profit,
and virtually everything that we [PETA] fight against is a result
of people trying to maximize their bottom line, maximize their
profits. And animals are bred to grow so large so fast that in the
case of chickens their legs can't support their weight and many

of those animals suffer from crippling leg deformities. They also suffer from heart attacks, they suffer from lung collapse. And because they're kept in such intense confinement on factory farms where in the case of chickens you see up to 10,000 animals warehoused in one system, then you see an enormous increase in mortality and disease. And to compensate for that chickens are fed seven times the amount of antibiotics that are

McLibel Case

In what became the longest-running legal trial in British history, fast-food company McDonald's took two activists, Dave Morris and Helen Steel, to trial for distributing fliers that made several claims against the food chain. These claims included accusing McDonald's of promoting unhealthy foods, helping to destroy rain forests for cattle grazing, exploiting children in their advertising, food poisoning, and participating in the mistreatment of animals used in their food. Although when a final ruling did come on June 19, 1997, three years after the case had first gone to trial, the judge declared that the defendants had not proven many of their allegations, the court did decide that McDonald's was guilty on several counts, including falsely advertising that their food was healthy, exploitation of children, antiunionism that resulted in low pay for workers, and being "culpably responsible" for animal cruelty. However, Justice Bell, who presided over the case, concluded that McDonald's had been libeled overall, and so Morris and Steel were ordered to pay the company £60,000 (around $100,000), a claim McDonald's later dropped, realizing Morris and Steel would never pay the sum.

Although feeling somewhat justified, Morris and Steel have not seen the end of the case, which is slated to go before the British House of Lords and the European Court of Human Rights. Nevertheless, the 1997 decision was devastating to McDonald's public relations. The "McLibel" case, as it has come to be known, has had implications in the United States, too. PETA, which had been supporting Morris and Steel's cause, put pressure on McDonald's to reform their treatment of animals especially and made suggestions as to how the animals should be treated. At first, McDonald's did not respond to letters from PETA, and this resulted in PETA's launching a campaign against the fast-food chain. The campaign was called off the next year when McDonald's began to comply with PETA's demands for better farm animal care.

fed to people or cows. So you do have this real problem with hormones in chicken flesh, antibiotics in animal flesh, which is passed on to us when we eat them.[6]

Furthermore, factory farming is hazardous to the environment, say animal rights activists and environmentalists. Manure from hog, poultry, and cattle farms has become an increasing problem, as the waste from these animals flows in high concentrations into water systems. In the past, when farm animals and plant crops were raised side by side in much less concentrated environments, such waste was often used for crop fertilizer. Today, most fertilizers are manufactured in chemical plants, and the feces and urine that are produced in factory farms have nowhere to go. Accumulated piles of animal excrement generate toxic fumes composed of hydrogen sulfide, carbon dioxide, ammonia, and methane; in addition to bacteria from this waste, the hormones and other medications given to the animals make their way into the water system. "Some 40 percent of the nitrogen and 35 percent of the phosphates contaminating the nation's rivers, lakes, and streams come from livestock wastes and feed fertilizers,"[7] says Fox, who also notes that nitrates have been shown to cause cancer in humans.

The process of slaughter is unnecessarily cruel.
It's not only how animals are treated in factory farms that upsets animal rights advocates, but how they are "processed" as well. The transport of farm animals is largely done by truck, but, as Fox notes, federal regulations only cover transportation by rail, and so the farm industry is largely free to ignore the care of their animals as they are shipped to the slaughterhouse. As a result, according to Fox, about 7 to 9 percent of the livestock suffer bruises and other injuries in transit, and some of the animals actually die before they reach the processing plant. Ironically, this is not only bad for the animals but it also undercuts profits. "The livestock industry loses $46 million annually from bruises on cattle and hogs," says Fox. "Federal inspectors condemn this bruised meat, enough to feed a

large city, *but only if they see it,* during cursory visual inspection."[8] Fox also adds that another $32 million is lost each year from hogs that become so stressed that they develop what is called pale, soft, exudative (PSE) meat that is unfit for consumption.

> • **How have demographics and economics changed the way modern farms operate? Should the government offer more subsidies and research grants to farmers and ranchers to change current animal husbandry practices?**

If the costs are so high, though, why are these methods of transportation used? According to a quote from one expert in the hog industry, "Death losses during transport are too high— amounting to more than $8 million per year. But it doesn't take a lot of imagination to figure out why we load as many hogs on a truck as we do. It's cheaper. So it becomes a moral issue. Is it right to overload a truck and save $.25 per head in the process, while the overcrowding contributes to the deaths of 80,000 hogs each year?"[9]

In the final step of the process, cattle, pigs, and chickens are killed in the slaughterhouse. The Humane Methods of Slaughter Act of 1978 (sometimes simply called the Humane Slaughter Act) stipulates that this is to be done in a humane manner, meaning that the animals should be given anesthesia and stunned before they are killed. (However, restrictions provided by the law do not apply to ritual slaughter, such as the killing of animals under Jewish kosher law, because that would violate religious freedom.) Once, it was workers wielding sledgehammers who stunned the animals; today, the job is done through automation. The animals are hung upside down by their hind legs on a moving rack, and then knocked unconscious by a stunning machine; the carotid arteries in their throats are then cut so they bleed to death in what would be a gruesome process for the faint of heart. The problem is that this assembly line can move so quickly (sometimes up to 250 cattle go by per hour) that the blows to the animals' heads sometimes miss. Harried workers, who are supposed to ensure that the animals are unconscious, often don't have time to check on the animals' status.

Thus, many cattle have their throats cut, their limbs removed, and their skin peeled back while they are still conscious.

> • **Many people in the United States have stopped eating veal because of publicity that shows how calves are treated to make the meat tender; yet these people often continue to eat other kinds of meat. At what point is it acceptable to eat animals, or do you feel it is never justifiable?**

The same fate awaits swine, but chickens are different. Because bird species are not covered by federal regulations, their method of death is not subject to federal guidelines. Legally, the birds can be slaughtered while still conscious, but processing plants still try to stun them so they aren't struggling when the mechanical blade cuts their throats. To immobilize the chickens, their heads are submerged in electrified water; however, to save energy costs, the current is sometimes too low to actually stun the chicken. Thus, the birds are sometimes still conscious when their throats are slit and their bodies are dumped in boiling water. "Inevitably," according to Mercy for Animals, "the blade misses some birds who then proceed to the next station on the assembly line, the scalding tank. Here they are submerged in boiling hot water. Birds missed by the killing blade are boiled alive. This occurs so commonly, affecting millions of birds every year, that the industry has a term for these birds. They are called 'redskins.'"[10]

If the conditions in factory farms are so appalling, as animal rights groups maintain, why are these animals not protected by the Animal Welfare Act, as laboratory animals are? As Nathan Runkle, the director of Mercy for Animals, comments:

> Farm animals are exempt from most cruelty laws . . . because factory farms couldn't exist if the animals were covered under the same laws that dogs or cats or other animals were. You can't confine six cats, seven cats, eight cats in a cage so small that they can't move. You'd be prosecuted for animal cruelty

with that, so the cruelty codes specifically exempt animals from such things as giving an animal wholesome air or exercise, which is really why factory farms can exist. . . . Anything that is considered standard agricultural practice is exempt, so that accounts for some of the worst animal abuses because these abuses are really standard.[11]

Because animal rights groups view the gap between the treatment of lab animals and pets versus the treatment of livestock animals as hypocritical, animal husbandry and meat processing have become one of their biggest concerns in recent years.

Hunting is a cruel activity.

Although the use of animals in agriculture has a long history, hunting animals for their meat, hides, and fur goes back to the very beginning of the human race. For centuries, hunting was necessary for human survival. Today, however, animal rights groups argue that the practice is no longer essential and, indeed, is practiced purely for entertainment and the thrill of the hunt. The result is that wildlife that should be allowed to roam free without harassment is unduly stressed, maimed, and killed. Of course, hunters have a different viewpoint. Daniel Cohen puts their perspective under the light of the antihunting position:

Hunters say that their activity gives them a chance to get out in the woods and enjoy nature, and to share the camaraderie of their friends. Of course, hiking, birdwatching, or nature photography could provide the same results. Hunters also insist that what they do is a "sport." That implies some sort of equal competition. The competition between a man with a high-powered rifle and a deer is hardly equal. If the man loses he goes home; if the deer loses it's dead.[12]

Death from a bullet or arrow might be less gruesome than processing in a slaughterhouse, but it can still result in a lot of pain for the animal. As Andrew Butler of PETA explains, "It's certainly not a very sure way of taking that animal's life. The animal can be wounded and die slowly and painfully in the woods, or it might take a couple of shots, they might be chased for hours upon end, causing a great deal of stress to that animal." [13] Another argument against animal hunting is that wildlife is often killed not for food but for trophies and other nonessential purposes, such as the illegal medicines trade. When a bear is killed, for example, the hunter will, in many cases, take it to a taxidermist to have the head mounted, or sometimes the entire body is stuffed and displayed. Certain bear organs, such as gall bladders, are also used to create medicines that are popularly sold in Asian countries. Bear bile is used in places such as China as a substitute for over-the-counter drugs commonly used in the United States that aren't always available overseas, such as Dristan and Viagra. Tiger bones and penises, to use two more examples, are similarly turned into medicines that are supposed to help improve virility and cure impotence.

Although many of these animal species are poached (hunted illegally), even dealers in exotic animals have come to realize that their wildlife supply will run out if such practices continue. They have therefore resorted to raising exotics themselves. For instance, there are now many bear ranches in China. As Alan Green writes in his revealing book *Animal Underworld:*

> Some five hundred farms sequester thousands of bears in warehouses [in China]. Each is outfitted with a metal girdle that contains a pouch to collect bile—the substance coveted by those in the East without ready access to Dristan, Viagra, or hemorrhoid potions. According to the Chinese government, the bile production from the seven or eight thousand bears that are caged helps relieve the threats to the remaining free-roaming bears, which would likely face slaughter for their gall bladders. This way, Chinese officials argue, the imperiled bear species are being saved. [14]

Such harvesting of animals is not limited to China, however. Hunting ranches have become increasingly common in the United States. These are places where both exotic and endemic (native) species are kept within fenced areas. For a fee, which can range up to several thousand dollars depending on the rarity of the species, hunters are guaranteed the chance to shoot the animal of their choice. Such ranches are becoming attractive to trophy hunters who are unable to shoot species such as giraffes and oryxes in Africa, where they are protected. Such hunts—sometimes known as "canned shoots"—are unfortunately still legal in the United States. As a reaction to canned shoots, in 1995, the Captive Exotic Animal Protection Act was proposed before the U.S. House of Representatives to stop such hunting, but it has failed to pass into law.

This is not to say that most hunters in the United States approve of such practices, though. Indeed, Green notes that the National Rifle Association (NRA) and Safari Club International are opposed to canned shoots because they violate the idea of a "fair chase." Health officials also worry that the importation and breeding of exotics can lead to the spread of diseases in both animals and people. This potential threat was made more apparent recently with the SARS (severe acute respiratory syndrome) scare, in which the disease is believed to have originally been transmitted to people in China who ate animals called civets. Criticism of the practice has therefore caused hunting ranches to be banned in some states, though it is still allowed in others, especially in the western United States.

> • **Do you feel that hunting is more humane than animal agriculture, since in hunting the animal is allowed to spend its life in the wild?**

Even the hunting of common animals such as deer can have negative consequences, however. As animal rights groups like to point out, hunters pursue the most impressive animals for their trophy collections. In the case of bucks (male deer), this means the animals with the largest antlers. Large antlers in deer indicate the healthiest animals, too, and so when hunters shoot the strongest bucks they are depleting the deer population of its healthiest animals, thus weakening the genetic makeup of the species as a whole. Still another problem comes with the type of hunting methods used and the skill of the hunter. Even hunters who use high-powered rifles can miss shooting an animal's internal organs, and when an animal is wounded, it can suffer for days before dying.

Bow hunting is an even less certain way of killing wildlife, and using dogs to catch species such as coyotes and foxes is a practice widely decried by animal rights groups. In the United States, coyotes, whose numbers are increasing because they are so adaptable to environmental changes caused by humans, are chased down by trained dogs that rip them to pieces. In the United Kingdom, a movement to end fox hunting, where foxes are chased down by dogs and armed men on horseback, is gaining support. One group that is fighting the practice in England is the Hunt Saboteur Association, whose members attempt to spoil hunts by blowing horns and laying down false trails to confuse the hunting dogs. In the United States, however, such practices have been made illegal by the Recreational Hunting Safety and Preservation Act of 1994.

Still another hunting method—trapping—has also been highly controversial. Traps, which are commonly used for smaller animals such as beaver and fox, typically break bones while keeping the animal alive and suffering. Some animals have been known to chew off their own legs to escape rather than remain in a trap. What is even sadder, say activists, is when an animal that the hunter did not mean to catch is trapped. According to Cathy Liss in *Animals and Their Legal Rights,* "Non-target animals caught in the traps include Bald and Golden Eagles, Great Horned Owls, Red-tailed Hawks, calves, fawns, deer, colts, lambs, goats, geese, and ducks."[15] Liss quoted one veterinarian who had treated trap wounds as saying: "Leghold traps inflict some of the worst, ugliest strangulation type leg wounds I see. I cannot imagine any greater terror for an animal than to be captured in one of these devices."[16]

The fur and leather industry also exploit animals for frivolous causes.

The fur industry has a long history of using traps to catch beavers, muskrats, foxes, lynx, otters, and many other species valued for their fur, which is then turned into clothing, such as women's coats. Not only is this practice responsible for causing great pain and suffering to wildlife, according to activists, but it is also very wasteful. According to the authors of *The Animal Rights Handbook*, "an estimated 17 million raccoons, beavers, bobcats, lynx, coyotes, muskrats, nutria, and other animals are trapped each year in the United States for fur."[17] It doesn't take just one animal to make an article of clothing, either: "To make a 40-inch coat, depending on the type, it takes 16 coyotes or 18 lynx or 60 mink, 45 opossums, 20 otters, 42 foxes, 40 raccoons, 50 sables, 8 seals, 50 muskrats, or 15 beavers."[18] This isn't including the number of "trash animals" (those that weren't intended to be caught), which is about double the amount of the desired animals caught per coat.

Just as with the agricultural industry, those in the fur industry have discovered that, in lieu of trapping, farms are a very cost-effective way to raise animals that are valued for their fur. Mink, chinchilla, and other types of fur farms are now a common way of obtaining fur, and the conditions on them are just as bad as on factory farms, say activists. Animals are kept in small cages inside large buildings, and, in order to hold down costs and protect the fur from damage, are killed in the least expensive way. This typically involves breaking their necks, poisoning them with gas, drowning or suffocating them, or the grisly practice of anal electrocution, which, according to Nathan Runkle of Mercy for Animals, "is really the most common way of killing chinchillas and it's also pretty common for killing foxes. . . . [All of these methods] really disregard the welfare of the animals." He added, "The fur industry is really just a violent and bloody industry that [exists] to produce a frivolous luxury item."[19] Many activists feel the same way about the leather industry, which is part and parcel of the institution of factory farming. *The Animal Rights Handbook* further notes that "leather is tanned with toxic chemicals, which find their way into streams and rivers, polluting them and killing wildlife."[20]

> • **How is killing an animal for its fur different from killing an animal for its meat? Is one more justified than the other?**

Vegetarianism provides an alternative.

The solution to all of the above problems, say many animal rights groups, is for people to change their lifestyles. Eliminating the use of fur, leather, and wildlife trophies would be simple enough if people changed their attitudes toward animals, since these products are not essential to human survival. Food, on the other hand, is a bigger problem. It is a daunting task to ask people to give up steak, hamburgers, pepperoni pizzas, fish sticks, pork chops, and innumerable other foods. But there are several reasons why we should, say pro–animal rights people, many of which have been outlined above. Vegetarians don't support the factory farm industry with their shopping dollars, which may help reduce the demand for meat products and, subsequently, eliminate the poor treatment of farm animals.

Getting rid of meat would also help the environment. Not only would there be no more manure runoff seeping into the water supply, but it takes much more acreage to support animal agriculture than plant agriculture. Activists often point out that the destruction of the Amazon rain forest is due largely to cattle farmers who hack down trees to create pastures for their animals. Because of the nature of rain forest soil, however, its fertility is tapped out after only a few years, and so more forest is hacked down. While crops such as corn and wheat also require space, they need much less acreage than that used for grazing. As Bruce Friedrich explains on the GoVeg Website:

> [T]he average vegan uses about 1/6 of an acre of land to satisfy his or her food requirements for a year; the average vegetarian who consumes dairy products and eggs requires about three times that, and the average meat-eater requires about 20 times that much land. We can grow a lot more food on an equal amount of land if we're not funneling the crops through animals.[21]

Finally, a vegetarian or vegan diet is simply healthier than a diet rich in meat. Typical Americans consume too much protein, cholesterol, and fat because we eat so many burgers, steaks, and chicken products. The result is an overweight nation that suffers from a high rate of heart ailments and other diet-related illnesses, including cancer. Vegetarians who eat no meat and vegans who eat neither meat nor dairy products maintain that they live healthier, longer lives that have less of a negative impact on animals and the environment.

> • **Would you be willing to give up eating meat and dairy products if it meant that no more animals would be harmed? Why or why not?**

Many of the uses to which animals have been put—as apparel and even as food—are not truly necessary for the survival of human beings. Because animals have the same desire to protect their lives that humans have, animal rights activists believe it is cruel to exploit them for frivolous uses.

Animals Should Be Used for Food and Clothing

Human beings are omnivores, which means that our natural diet includes a mix of food from animals and plants. If one accepts the current theories of humankind's evolution, *Homo sapiens*' origins can be found in early primate species that lived in trees in Africa. When climactic changes caused many of those trees to be replaced with open savannahs, the diets of these primates, which had been primarily vegetarian, began to incorporate meat as a matter of necessity. The result of this switch in lifestyle was a dramatic impact on the course of evolution, according to some scholars, who say that a meat diet helped increase brain size in our ancestors and was the basis for new social behaviors. As Craig B. Stanford asserts in his book *The Hunting Apes: Meat Eating and the Origins of Human Behavior*, "The origins of human intelligence are linked to the acquisition of meat, especially through the cognitive capacities necessary for the strategic sharing of meat with fellow group members."[1] Studying other primates, such as chimps, and supplementing this information with what anthropologists know about early humans, Stanford theorizes that meat was the first object of barter for early peoples: "Underlying the nutritional aspect of getting meat, part of the social fabric of the community is revealed in the dominance displays, the tolerated theft, and the bartered meat for sexual access. The end of the hunt is often only the beginning of a whole other arena of social interaction."[2]

Thus, say some, the introduction of meat into our diet played a large part in forming early social structures, a cohesive society. Later, as humanity developed agriculture, animals became even more important. Domesticated animals were a source of food and labor. Without animals, many people believe, agriculture would not have come about, and, therefore, human civilization would not have developed. Dan Murphy, a former journalist who is now vice president for public affairs at the American Meat Institute, further explains the importance of animals in agriculture:

> In any point in time, at any point in history, on any continent, among any people that we're aware of in the entire existence of the human race [there was no group of people] who were truly vegetarian. . . . From the days that people first crawled out of the trees and started hunting and gathering to the more advanced, agriculturally based societies in previous millennia to virtually every indigenous group of people on every continent and every time in history have used either wild animals that were hunted or trapped, fished, netted, captured, as supplement to their food base, or, in the more advanced societies, animals were domesticated in a very symbiotic way to not only provide the work as work animals on farms but as food animals and as a readily available source of fertilizer manure for the vegetable and grain crops that were grown. That is universal. . . .

In fact, one of the few examples where it wasn't the case—the aboriginal people of Australia—there really were no large animals capable of being domesticated on that continent because of their geologic isolation back how many millions of years ago. They are the one race of people on Earth that never progressed beyond the stone age. Think about it. It's not that they're unintelligent; it's not that they were incapable of the intellectual progress that you would say characterizes most advanced societies we know about. The very simple, plain truth is that all members of the aboriginal tribes had to spend all of their time gathering and acquiring food for themselves. They had no livestock which would allow them to do large-scale farming. As a result there was never a food surplus, so there could never be anyone in their society who could devote themselves to arts or culture or science.[3]

> • **Meat has always been part of the human diet, yet vegetarians say we should abandon it completely. In what ways might our world change if nobody ate meat any longer? Would this change human civilization as well as the environment?**

Modern agriculture helps society in many ways.

For thousands of years, animal farming existed in a virtually unchanged form. Many people raised their own cattle, goats, sheep, pigs, and poultry on private farms and then sold the animals to their neighbors or at the marketplace. The livestock grazed on open land or were fed by hand, and herds were small by today's standards. This way of life continued through the early twentieth century. However, after World War II, the agrarian lifestyle began to change dramatically in industrialized nations like the United States. More and more people began to move off the farms and into cities and the growing suburbs, where jobs were more plentiful. As one commentator on the issue wrote, "It is worth remembering that just before World War II one in four of us lived on a farm; now it is one in 50. What do most urban and suburban kids know about animals, other than what they see in cartoons?"[4]

The world's population also began to explode, and this naturally brought about a sharp increase in the demand for food. The rise of what animal rights activists label "factory farms"—what those in the industry simply call "modern farming"—really took off in the 1980s, when technology vastly improved the efficiency of agricultural operations and made it possible for a shrinking number of farmers to provide a growing number of customers meat products at an affordable price. So, contrary to the animal rights groups' assertion that modern techniques are motivated purely by money, farmers and ranchers would claim that new methods have developed out of necessity.

Although animal rights advocates like to describe today's modern agricultural facility as a "factory farm," those in the industry generally object to the term. Kay Johnson, vice president of the American Agricultural Alliance, is one of them:

> Let me just say that the term "factory farm" has become quite a buzzword out there. It was created, I'm sure, to conjure up all sorts of negative ideas when you think of sweatshops and people working hard and being treated poorly and so forth. . . . Factory workers, factory farms, you have this image of dirty and hard work and hot and sweaty. It's a buzzword that basically was created to conjure up these same ideas about animals that are raised for food today. Farming certainly has changed over the years through science, through technology—also because of change in demographics—throughout all of our industries. Fewer and fewer people have wanted to work on farms; more and more people have flocked to businesses in cities and technology industries where they can make a lot more money and have more defined hours and not be committed to a lifestyle.
>
> Through technology, we as an industry—agriculture—

have had to learn how to do things differently. They've had to learn how to apply technology to their industry, their businesses, in order to thrive and basically survive when it's hard to find employees who want to work and commit their lifestyle to farms and food production. . . . We refer to it as modern agriculture as opposed to "factory farms." . . . The image that I come up with when I think of "factory farms" is that there are no people involved anymore, that animals are just put into buildings, put into cages, put into systems, and there's no longer human contact. That couldn't be farther from the truth. There is still a huge amount of human contact and commitment and responsibility and stewardship to these animals by the people who not only own the animals but who are also there working on a daily basis with the animals.[5]

Animal rights activists also like to paint a picture of the meat industry as a business that is primarily operated by large, impersonal corporations. In reality, Johnson explains, U.S. Department of Agriculture (USDA) figures indicate that "over 98.5 percent of the farms [in America] today are still owned by families and that is a fact that gets lost and is never mentioned by any of the activists."[6]

- **With the huge explosion of the human population over the last hundred years or so, do you feel that it is necessary for the meat industry to become more efficient in order to meet demands for food?**

Housing, care, and slaughter of animals for meat is done humanely.

The animal liberationists' argument that farmers and ranchers are unconcerned about illness and suffering in their animals is patently false, according to Murphy and Johnson, if for no other reason than the fact that sick and stressed animals damage the meat product and, therefore, the farmer's bottom line. Even stressed or bruised animals can be deemed unfit for market. Stress in pigs, for example, results in PSE—pale, soft, exudative pork—that is not fit for human consumption, and DFD—dark, firm, dry meat—can occur in cattle that are mishandled. As Murphy puts it:

> So that's where we start on this whole issue, that there is in fact a very clear and very powerful and very pervasive economic incentive for farmers and ranchers and hog producers to take care of their livestock and properly manage their animals because that's how they make money. Any more than, let's say, a farmer who has a citrus orchard and didn't bother irrigating his trees and didn't prune them in the off season and didn't bother managing the growth of underbrush and weeds so that his trees got the maximum nutrients from the soil. Why would you do that? Why would you be in business so that you didn't try to maximize your return? Number one, you wouldn't stay in business very long because you wouldn't be competitive, and number two, it simply runs contrary to the nature of *any* commercial enterprise. You don't do it if you're not making money.[7]

- **How much loss of a product due to animals dying or becoming too stressed would be acceptable to a farmer or rancher trying to make a profit in his or her business? Is some sacrifice worth it in order to make the business run more efficiently?**

Murphy went on to note that cattle raised for their meat spend all but the final 90 to 100 days of their lives grazing in pastures. Their last months are spent in what is called a feedlot, where, he maintains, the animals are given plenty of room to move around. As he points out, "You wouldn't want a 1,200 pound steer to be getting angry that they can't move around."[8] Pigs, he admits, do spend their entire lives indoors these days. But the purpose of this is to keep the animals safer and better cared for, especially pregnant sows and their piglets. By taking good care of their pigs, hog farmers ensure that nearly 100 percent of them survive, whereas if they were allowed to roam freely there would be a much higher mortality rate, especially for piglets. Murphy poses the question:

> Would they be better off running around outdoors and many of the piglets in every litter would end up dying? Is that better? Is that natural? Those are almost philosophical questions that are really different from asking the question [of whether] today's farmers, ranchers, and livestock producers do the best job with the systems they have in place designed for efficiency and designed for maximum survivability of the animal. Do they do the best job of maintaining the living conditions for the animals in those systems? I think the answer is yes, on a general basis.[9]

As for poultry—chickens, generally speaking—these birds have been domesticated for so many centuries that they are much more suited to life indoors than out, says Murphy. Although he admits that laying hens are kept in cages, except for some "free-range" hens whose eggs consequently cost more, he adds that broiler chickens (those raised expressly for their meat) are allowed to walk about in large indoor quarters. As for practices such as tail-docking in pigs and debeaking for chickens, these are practiced to a greater or lesser extent depending on the farm. Tail-docking is done to keep pigs from getting infections after they bite each other on the tail, as sometimes happens, and, as explained earlier, debeaking keeps chickens from pecking and wounding one another while still allowing them to eat normally. Though such operations might cause temporary pain and stress to the animal, long-term health and safety is the goal. As with any industry, there are sometimes unscrupulous people whose farms are not clean and well maintained, but they are in the minority, asserts Murphy.

• **If you were a farmer, would you believe the government should be allowed to change your business practices for the sake of animal rights? How much should government be involved in your working life?**

Overall, concludes Johnson, the agricultural industry is doing what it can to ensure the welfare of farm animals and is working all the time to improve conditions. She cautions, too, that people should not anthropomorphize animals: We should not think that because *we* might consider certain living conditions uncomfortable for ourselves that the same would be true for the animals:

> You have a lot of science that goes into what has been the best housing system to have the proper ventilation and to have the proper disposal of waste and the proper space requirements for each of these animals. When you and I look at these animals we can't just apply our human feelings and say, "Oh, I don't know if I'd like to live like that." Well, you know, many of these animals live in groups, they live in flocks. Having more space is not necessarily good, and that's where it's important that we look at what the science is. . . . We have to apply science and not emotion.[10]

Hunting is not the cruel practice opponents claim it is.

Because it involves actively pursuing and killing an animal, hunting can often be an even more emotional issue than meat processing for many people. There are many people who have no qualms about buying packaged meat in a grocery store, but ask them to personally shoot and butcher a wild deer and they will generally protest the idea vehemently. Animal rights activists view hunters as more bloodthirsty because they are involved firsthand in the killing, but hunters themselves take a very different view. For them, hunting is a way of life, and it can even have spiritual aspects. Hunting provides a sense of camaraderie, even among those who don't know each other well but share a mutual love of the sport. As one hunter comments, "True hunters, whatever their differences in geography, culture, gender, or experience, are kindred spirits, a tribe united by a shared love for what [conservationist and author] Paul Shepard, employing double entendre, calls the 'sacred game.' . . . It's a love, this ancient game, that cuts so deep yet remains so inexplicable as to seem almost instinctive."[11] Many hunters therefore cringe at the thought of calling hunting just a "sport" or "recreational activity." It is much more to them, as one writer notes:

> Hunting, however much a recreational activity, can only be fully comprehended if it is understood as a complex cultural phenomenon closely linked to naturalistic values, one's identity, and the American family. To the nonhunter, hunting is often viewed as just another recreational activity. But research clearly indicates that there is something much deeper. Hunting is an important social and psychological activity for hunters. Hunting is a powerful and meaningful pursuit, seemingly above and beyond other forms of recreational activities. . . . Hunting is not just recreation.[12]

> • **If you hunted and shot an animal for its meat, would you appreciate the food you ate more than if you had bought it in a supermarket?**

Hunters also generally feel that they are more attuned to nature than nonhunters are. Even the revered naturalist Aldo Leopold seemed to appreciate this characteristic of the hunter, writing in his well-known *Sand County Almanac,* "The deer hunter habitually watches the next bend; the duck hunter watches the skyline; the bird hunter watches the dog; the non-hunter does not watch. When the deer hunter sits down he sits where he can see ahead, and with his back to something. The duck hunter sits where he can see overhead, and behind something. The nonhunter sits where he is comfortable."[13] It is because they are more in sync with their natural surroundings that hunters can appreciate nature more than most people do, they maintain. For this reason, hunters claim that they have become instrumental in protecting natural spaces for future generations. This tradition goes back to the time of President Theodore Roosevelt. An avid hunter himself, Roosevelt recognized in the early 1900s that wild game was quickly disappearing in the United States, and so he set aside huge tracts of land as national forests to help provide space for these animals.

Today, many hunting organizations are more involved than ever in wildlife conservation. For example, the Rocky Mountain Elk Foundation (RMEF), an organization of elk (wapiti) hunters, works with private landowners and government agencies to protect land from development, is involved with education and wildlife research projects to help people understand the needs of elk and other animals, and also participates in wildlife and habitat management. "Understanding what the land needs is the key to wildlife conservation," according to the RMEF. "The Rocky Mountain Elk Foundation cooperates with state and federal agencies, other conservation groups and private industry to discover not only what the habitat needs in order to sustain healthy wildlife populations, but also how to provide it. RMEF State Project Advisory Committees bring together representatives of all these groups to recommend the highest priority conservation projects for RMEF funding."[14] Just a few of the many other groups that work toward the same goal include Ducks Unlimited, the Mule Deer Foundation, the National Shooting Sports Foundation, the National Wild Turkey Foundation, Safari Club International, and the U.S. Sportsmen's Alliance.

Such organizations maintain that hunting, far from being unnecessary, is doing a great deal to ensure that wildlife will still be around for future generations to enjoy. As for charges that hunting is a cruel sport for animals, many hunters would say that it is no crueler than butchering cattle, pigs, or chickens at a slaughterhouse. Trophy hunting, such as for deer antlers or large bears, is viewed as acceptable as long as it is done in a way that is as humane as possible and honors the law. On the other hand, "canned hunts" on hunting ranches are excoriated by people

Safari Club International Conservation Program

In North America, SCI Foundation focuses on wildlife management for big game species and wildlife habitat conservation. We help support excellent research, science-based wildlife management practices, and conservation advocacy with the federal and state governments.

In Alaska, the most difficult challenge is the decline in moose populations due to lack of grazing areas and predation by black bears. We're working here to support the development of private land wildlife management. More than 33 million acres of privately-held wildlife habitat are currently closed to sport hunting and reserved only for subsistence hunting. Wildlife management programs that generate significant income to landowners while conserving wildlife and increasing hunting opportunities is a primary goal.

. . . Chronic Wasting Disease has become a concern and is a priority for SCI Foundation. We support state and federal research, monitoring and management programs and hunter education classes that encourage sportsmen to participate in the surveillance efforts needed to protect deer and elk threatened by CWD.

Mule deer populations are declining due to a number of complex wildlife management issues. At our American Wilderness Leadership School near Jackson Hole, Wyoming, SCI Foundation hosted a Western Association Mule Deer task force workshop for state fish and wildlife agencies in 2002 and will do so again in 2003 to help them learn more about this problem and how to solve it.

In Mexico, SCI Foundation funded and managed the five-year jaguar initiative that led to the landscape scale habitat management plan for jaguar in the Yucatan Peninsula. This successful program is expanding into Belize and Guatemala.

Source: Available online at *http://www.scifirstforhunters.org/content/website/about/ conservation/northamericaprogram/*.

who consider themselves "true hunters." David Peterson, for one, asserts that shooting an animal on a ranch is in no sense real hunting:

> By self-definition, any "hunt" that requires no hunting is no hunt at all. Yet the privatization of wildlife for profit— euphemized as "alternative livestock ranching" (or, in the vernacular of some regions, "game farming")—is a boomer growth industry. Moreover, it's eagerly endorsed by state departments of agriculture throughout Canada and the American West (with the noble exception of Wyoming)— even as it's decried on pragmatic as well as moral grounds by ethical hunters, including a majority of trophy hunters and professional wildlife managers.[15]

• **Do you feel hunting is a way of life that should be preserved, or is it an antiquated hobby that encourages senseless killing? How important is hunting in maintaining the balance of nature in the wild now that many predator animals are gone?**

People who shoot animals on such ranches are the ones who do not appreciate or understand true hunting, and those who consider themselves real hunters do not in any way wish to be grouped with them. It is, many hunters admit, a real problem, but it should not be used as an argument for the banning of all hunting. Groups such as Safari Club International (SCI) also resent being accused of killing off endangered species. As SCI attests, animal rights groups such as PETA "falsely [assert] that 'hunters kill hundreds of rare, endangered and threatened animals annually.' Nothing could be further from the truth! Legal hunting is done on a permit basis through which populations are managed by government biologists."[16]

Those who consider themselves environmentalists and conservationists in the United States often laud and honor the traditional way of life of Native American tribes, a lifestyle that seemed to make it possible for people to live in balance with nature. Yet one does not hear groups such as PETA attacking Native Americans for their traditional practices of hunting and fishing, eating meat, and wearing animal fur and leather. It has apparently become politically correct for them to attack modern-day Americans for the same activities, some hunters complain. Properly done, hunting can be a humane activity that can even benefit wildlife by preventing overpopulation and by garnering the support of organizations that wish to pursue hunting for generations to come.

The fur industry responds to critics.

Far from what animal rights activists say about the fur industry destroying the environment and perpetrating various cruelties on fur farms, those in the industry state that the opposite is true. According to Fur Commission USA,

> No furs from endangered species are sold in the United States. Fur sold in the U.S. comes from one of two sources: from fur farms or from trapping regulated by state governments. As wildlife habitat has given way to civilization, it has become vital to manage animal populations not only for the protection of people but for the survival of the animals themselves. That's why trapping is recognized, endorsed and regulated by government as an important element in proper wildlife management.[17]

Fur is also a renewable resource that helps reduce human waste because animals such as mink and fox eat by-products of meat and grain that otherwise would have been thrown away as unfit for human consumption. As for animals kept on fur farms, they are treated as well as possible because, as any farmer involved in the industry would agree, quality furs come only from the healthiest animals. "America's family fur farmers have adopted a rigorous program of humane care guidelines based on technical input from veterinarians, nutritionists, furbearer biologists and animal scientists," according to Fur Commission USA. "The fur industry's Merit Award certification program requires veterinary inspection of fur farms. Today more than 95% of domestic fur production in the U.S. comes from certified farms which have passed inspection by an independent licensed veterinarian."[18]

Fur farmers further emphasize that fur is a natural substance that does not harm the environment, whereas synthetic materials that are in wide use today as substitutes for furs and leathers cause a great deal of damage. As furrier Mark Schumacher notes,

> If the planet Earth is going to be saved from destruction, we cannot rely on synthetic clothing for our future existence. The extraction of oil is killing the environment by the spilling of oil and the taking of the animals' habitat or home. The processing plants used to make artificial fibers pollute the air (acid rain and the depletion of ozone), streams and rivers and create toxic waste. The clothing (fake furs, nylons, rayons, and polyester) made from these synthetic products fill up our landfills and is not biodegradable.[19]

- **Fur, say those in the industry, is a renewable resource, whereas many manmade fibers—such as rayon and Dacron®—use environmentally harmful chemicals in the production process; even raising cotton can be harmful, since pesticides are used on the crops. If animals such as mink are raised humanely with little effect on the environment, how would you feel about wearing a fur coat? Is wearing leather more or less moral than wearing fur?**

As for how the animals are killed on fur farms, although groups like PETA shock the public with stories about anal electrocution, the preferred method, say fur farmers, is actually euthanasia through the use of carbon monoxide, which causes the animal no stress and is as painless as putting a dog or cat to sleep. Since the meat of animals such as mink and fox is not palatable to people, it is instead sold to such places as zoos and aquariums, or used as crab bait or to make fertilizer; mink oil (which comes from the fat of the animal) can be used as a leather conditioner or in cosmetics. So, although the primary goal of fur farms is pelt production, no part of the animals raised is wasted. Overall, those in the fur industry would argue that harvesting fur is a clean and humane farming practice that is actually beneficial to the environment.

Meat is an important part of our diet.

Biologically and physiologically speaking, human beings are by nature omnivorous. This means that we have evolved to live on a diet combining both meats and vegetables, and we have the dentition to prove it. The canines and incisors in our mouths are designed to tear into meat and not for chewing plants, which is the job of our molars. Because we are omnivores, medical doctors have long recommended that we eat a balanced diet that includes some meat products, which are a good source of essential proteins. The U.S. Department of Agriculture, while promoting a diet high in vegetables, fruits, and grains, also includes in its suggested diet two to three servings of meat, poultry, fish, eggs, or beans and nuts a day, as well as two to three servings of milk, yogurt, or cheese, which are, of course, derived from animals. These foods are important, according to the USDA, because they contain "B vitamins, iron, and zinc. The other foods in this group—dry beans, eggs, and nuts—are similar to meats in providing protein and most vitamins and minerals." [20]

While almost all doctors feel that eating meat and dairy products is fine, some physicians have gone even further. The most famous of these is the late Dr. Robert C. Atkins, whose popular Atkins Diet recommends that people eat a diet rich in meat proteins and low in carbohydrates. To Atkins, many people's health problems today are not the result of eating too many meats but because people eat a lot of sugar, processed flour, and junk foods. Because the body naturally burns off carbohydrates before other sources of energy, says Atkins, those who eat a lot of them tend to be overweight. Eating meats, even those high in fat, along with vegetables low in carbohydrates and a few fruits, actually improves many people's health. "I'm ready to tell you that if you want to be slim and vigorous," Atkins writes, "you can eat like a king or queen. . . . On the Atkins diet, you can eat the natural, healthy animal and vegetable foods that people ate and grew robust on in centuries past. You don't have to be austere or peculiar. You don't have to eat like a rabbit; you can eat like a human being."[21]

This is, essentially, the gist of what those who advocate meat eating are saying: Eating animals is not inhumane or immoral. It's natural.

> • **Do you feel more health problems in people are caused by eating too much meat or by eating too many sugars and processed food snacks?**

Those who advocate ending the use of animals for food and clothing are ignoring thousands of years of tradition. Human beings have always been omnivorous and have always used animals as a means to their own survival.

Animals Should Not Be Used for Entertainment

Humanity has made use of all types of animals over the millennia, but it is only in recent history that animals have become performers, entertainers, companions, and objects for display. Although dogs and cats have been domesticated for centuries, for most of human history, they were viewed merely as working animals. Dogs were bred to herd cattle, sheep, and goats, and in some parts of the world, to haul small wagons; cats were useful for getting rid of pests such as mice and rats, and they generally stayed outdoors. It is a relatively recent development in our culture that dogs, cats, birds, and even fish, reptiles, and insects, have become our "companions."

Exotic animals were largely ignored in the West, although in some Eastern countries, animals that we might consider exotic, such as the elephant, were—and still are—used for labor. It wasn't until the nineteenth century that circuses, zoos, and other entertainment venues began to use exotics to draw crowds of paying customers. Animals don't always have to be exotic, of course, to earn money for businesses. Rodeos, dog races, horse-racing, and illegal dog fights and cockfights are also businesses that animal rights groups say exploit animals.

- **How do you think people's attitudes about zoos have changed over the last few decades?**

Zoos do not let animals live as they would in the wild.

The recorded history of zoos goes back to about 2300 B.C. Archaeologists discovered a stone tablet in the remains of the city of Ur, part of the Sumerian civilization, which describes a collection of rare animals. Centuries later, it is known that the Egyptian pharaohs also had such collections. These menageries of interesting species were usually brought back from conquests in foreign lands and presented for the amusement of rulers from Rome to India to Europe. Access to the animals was often restricted to members of royalty. By Victorian times, England was seeing the creation of zoological gardens, the first being the Regent's Park Zoo in London, which was opened by the Zoological Society of London in 1828. Zoos became very popular and spread to the United States, where the first zoo, the Philadelphia Zoo, opened in 1874. The Bronx Zoo, the National Zoo, Zoo Atlanta, and the San Diego Zoo followed in the early 1900s.

To fill the cages at these zoos with animals, trappers were hired to capture live wildlife in Africa and other locations. Animals were typically kept in stark cement cages surrounded by metal bars, settings that were far less comfortable than their original homes. But zoos were not overly concerned about the comfort of their animals at the time. If a particular animal died, they would simply retrieve another one from the wild. Problems with this approach began to arise by the mid-twentieth century, however, when the decreasing number of available wildlife began to pose a supply problem. That was when captive breeding programs began to take hold. Zoos cooperated with each other, trading animals so that they could be bred with one another and so the supply of exotics would be assured. This program later evolved into the Species Survival Plan. Zoos also began to realize that animals were more likely to breed if they were housed in more natural enclosures. Exhibit design, led by such people as Dr. Heini Hediger, who directed zoos in Basel and Zurich, Switzerland, in the 1940s and 1950s, also became important. Jon Coe and Grant Jones, who led the way in the 1970s in the creation of "landscape immersion exhibits" that tried to make zoo visitors feel as if they were part of the exhibit, became well-known exhibit architects.

Today, zoos accredited by the American Zoo and Aquarium Association (AZA) aver that although they are still places for public entertainment, their main mission is the conservation of endangered wildlife and the education of the public about wildlife concerns. To become accredited by the AZA, zoos are inspected for their treatment, care, and housing of resident species. Zoos are also subject to federal regulations set down by the Animal Welfare Act. Despite such oversight, many animal rights groups see a lot of problems with zoos, including limits on the freedom of animals, which are confined to exhibit areas much smaller than the spaces they would inhabit in the wild; unsuitable living conditions; and zoo breeding programs that are motivated by a desire to produce baby animals that will attract more customers.

In *Animal Equality: Language and Liberation,* author Joan Dunayer asserts that despite the insistence of zoos that their exhibits now emulate natural living conditions, the enclosures are far from adequate:

> While zoo visitors experience what the industry calls "habitat immersion," the inmates experience exhibit imprisonment.

Their worlds extend no farther than transparent plastic walls, invisible electrified wire, or scarcely perceptible mesh. "Cold concrete walls" [Dunayer is quoting an August 10, 1996, *Boston Globe* article by Vicki Croke] surround the animals kept inside the Tropical Forest at Franklin Park Zoo (Boston). Beyond spectators' view, conditions are worse. Hidden behind exhibits with expansive names like African Plains, you'll find barred concrete cells.[1]

Wild animals restricted to limited space, point out activists, become vulnerable to psychological disorders caused by boredom and lack of stimulation. Animals exhibit this boredom in a way similar to animals confined to factory farms: They pace, pull out their hair or feathers obsessively, walk around in circles, bite the bars of their cages, or become listless. This is true, says Vicki Croke in *The Modern Ark, The Story of Zoos: Past, Present and Future,* even in the best-designed zoos:

> Zoo officials vehemently disagree, but according to a recent survey conducted by the Born Free Foundation (a British charity that monitors animals in captivity), mental illness among zoo animals is rampant. Somewhat anecdotal, the 1993 study took three years to complete and involved one hundred zoos. The group says it found a bulimic gorilla in Barcelona, bulimic chimps in Sacramento, a psychotic baboon in Cyprus and a bear that constantly pulled its hair out in Rome. The director of the study said, "Our evidence confirms that deprived of their natural environment, social structures and outlets for many of the skills for which they have naturally evolved, animals exhibit abnormal behavior."[2]

Michael W. Fox, writing in *Inhumane Society,* goes even further in indicting the practice of confining animals to zoos:

"Regarding the claim that the best zoos are helping save species from extinction by breeding them in captivity, it may be best to let them become extinct if there is no place for them in the wild." [3]

- **Do you believe that a wild animal can be happy in a zoo if it is given enough food, water, and shelter, or does it need to have freedom in the wild to be truly content?**

Perhaps the most damning condemnation of zoo breeding programs came with the 1999 publication of Alan Green's *Animal Underworld: Inside America's Black Market for Rare and Exotic Species.* In it, Green accuses zoos of selling off "surplus" and otherwise unwanted animals to dealers, who then sell them to "roadside zoos" (zoos not accredited by the AZA and therefore not subject to rules about the care or maintenance of their animals), hunting ranches, or auctions that sell to private collectors who want exotic animals as pets. An elaborate black market has sprung up in the United States, according to Green, and zoos play an unwitting part in it. When zoos have no room for an animal (a chronic problem around the country), they advertise the animals either in a trade journal called the *Animal Finders' Guide* or the AZA monthly newsletter *Animal Exchange,* which are read widely by dealers in exotic animals.

Although zoos are supposed to sell their animals only to accredited zoos or animal sanctuaries, this is not always what happens. Disreputable dealers will participate in a kind of shell game, selling and reselling animals at various destinations until the paperwork becomes so convoluted—or misplaced—by federal agents charged with tracking the trade of animals across state lines, that the animals' origins become a mystery and they become victims of apparently legal sales to roadside zoos or hunting ranches. Reports Green:

State veterinary officials estimate that only 10 to 15 percent of nonfarm animals moving across state lines do so legally—that is, with the proper import permits and truthful health certificates. It's no secret that coyote pups are paid for in cash and driven to places where their ownership is prohibited. That truckloads of animals are delivered to backwoods foxpens under the cover of darkness. That venomous reptiles are sent via parcel carriers in boxes marked "glassware." That bears vanish. That giraffes disappear. That mountain lions are sent to fictitious wildlife centers. That tiny monkeys are hidden amid a bed of newspaper and claimed as squirrels when passed through airline cargo terminals. That animals travel with no paperwork, bogus paperwork, or paperwork that intentionally obscures details of the transaction.[4]

Green, who spent years investigating the animal black market, does not directly blame zoo officials for this black market trade, saying that reputable zoos usually intend to find good homes for their surplus animals. Rather, he asserts that the illegal shenanigans of exotic animal dealers have become so complex that it is difficult for anyone to find out what happens to all the animals that leave zoos. Animal traders routinely transport their charges through many states in order to create a labyrinthine paper trail. "Despite liberal open-records laws in most states," he writes, "collecting health certificates was proving to be difficult, in some cases nearly impossible."[5] Sometimes he would run into state-employed veterinarians who would refuse to produce documents because they contained "sensitive information."

Green further contends that animals that are not considered endangered, such as some species of common bears, reptiles, and insects, are not treated as carefully by zoos. These animals are considered "nothing but seasonal props—disposable exhibits that in no way further the zoos' stated missions of conservation and education."[6] His research revealed that exotic birds have been sold to casinos, reptiles

Worth more dead than alive

Experts estimate that captive tigers in the United States outnumber all tigers living in the wild. With live tigers going for a meager $1,000 these great beasts are worth more slaughtered and sold on the international black market.

Some of the highest reported prices for various tiger products by country:

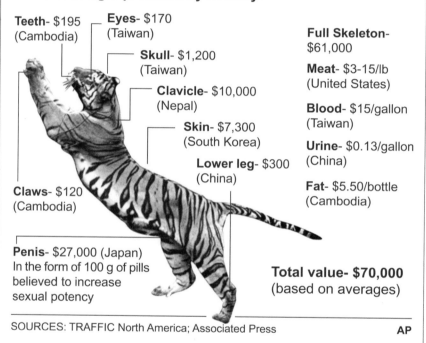

Teeth- $195
(Cambodia)

Eyes- $170
(Taiwan)

Skull- $1,200
(Taiwan)

Clavicle- $10,000
(Nepal)

Skin- $7,300
(South Korea)

Lower leg- $300
(China)

Claws- $120
(Cambodia)

Penis- $27,000 (Japan)
In the form of 100 g of pills
believed to increase
sexual potency

Full Skeleton-
$61,000

Meat- $3-15/lb
(United States)

Blood- $15/gallon
(Taiwan)

Urine- $0.13/gallon
(China)

Fat- $5.50/bottle
(Cambodia)

Total value- $70,000
(based on averages)

SOURCES: TRAFFIC North America; Associated Press   **AP**

Although animal rights supporters would argue that wild animals, such as tigers, are inherently priceless, a thriving black market is more than willing to put a price tag on animals—or, more precisely, animal parts. As this Associated Press chart indicates, the body of a single tiger, with its parts distributed to the most lucrative market, can sell for as much as $70,000—a massive sum when one considers that live tigers generally sell for only about $1,000.

sold to pet stores, and zoo reindeer used by private companies to promote Christmas sales. The result, as with the case of the Little Rock Zoo in Arkansas, which was temporarily suspended from accreditation by the AZA in 1999 for such practices, is that some zoos are reprimanded. But the practice still goes on in some cases.

Despite their declared mission to save endangered animals, zoos violate the basic rights of animals to live freely in natural environments as they were intended, say activists. For this reason, zoos are not considered viable solutions for the cause of wildlife conservation. However, as entertainment venues for the public, they are still generally seen as better than some of the alternatives.

- **If zoos were no longer places for the public to be entertained but instead became more like animal reserves, would people still support them?**

Circuses and marine parks subject animals to cruel treatment.

Vociferous campaigns against zoos are not too common these days because they are widely regarded by the public to be at least bearable homes for wildlife. Therefore, animal rights groups such as PETA have devoted much more attention to circuses and marine parks, such as Sea World and Marineland, which deliberately train animals to perform stunts for the public's entertainment with the intention of making money. While it's true that it was once common for zoos to have performing chimps and birds as part of their programs, this practice is generally not considered appropriate at zoos today. On the other hand, a big part of what makes a circus entertaining is the animal shows. To accomplish this, animals such as elephants, lions, and tigers undergo months of training under the guidance of animal trainers using, according to PETA, unethically cruel methods. PETA says that trainers use ropes, chains, bats, whips, metal pipes, muzzles, and bullhooks (also known as ankuses). (Bullhooks are long metal devices with hooks on the end that are used to beat and intimidate elephants into submission.) In some cases, PETA claims, animals that have gone out of control have been shot outright.

According to Mercy for Animals, investigations into

One Opinion on How to Train Elephants

In *I Loved Rogues*, elephant trainers George "Slim" Lewis and Byron Fish wrote:

Circus animals are performers, and training them depends on a certain amount of rough treatment.

What is true of training for performance is even more true of the basic discipline that must be established before an elephant can work or act. It isn't kept in a cage, and, while it is chained much of the time, there are many occasions when it walks at liberty with only the respect it pays its handler to keep it in check. It is absolutely essential, therefore, that the animal must have this respect for its handler; and to get down to blunt facts, this quality begins with fear: fear of punishment and discomfort.

A good stout stick should be used, and it should have a sharp prod on the end of it to keep the elephant from turning its head.

[Teaching an elephant to lie down is] done by gradually tightening the chain, a few inches at a time, until the elephant is supporting its weight entirely on the front and hind legs that are free. It is very tiring for a bull to hold up its mass in this manner. When the handler sees it weakening, he gives the command, "Down! Come on down."

The command is repeated until the elephant obeys. Just before it gives in, it will show signs of fear and defeat. Its eyes will bulge and its bowels become loose and watery as they are emptied several times.

When the elephant finally surrenders and falls over on its side, it knows it is comparatively helpless and that it has lost a psychological battle.

Source: Available online at *http://circuses.com/bullhook.html*.

circuses have revealed that physical punishment of animals is commonplace:

> Physical punishment has long been the standard training method for animals in circuses. Some species are less able to adapt to training techniques than others, and as a result suffer great stress during training sessions. Some animals are drugged to make them "manageable," and some have their teeth removed. The AWA [Animal Welfare Act] puts no restrictions on what training methods may be used, and, according to former animal trainer Pat Derby, "After 25 years of observing and documenting circuses, I know there are no kind animal trainers."[7]

Living conditions for animals at circuses are also abysmal, attest animal liberationists. Elephants are chained, tigers and bears kept in small cages, and baby animals separated too early from their mothers in order to begin training. Furthermore, PETA has claimed that, unlike at zoos, many of the animals used in circuses are still captured from the wild. "The animal slave trade from Africa still persists to this day," according to Andrew Butler of PETA, "where you have game dealers who go out, they round up families of elephants, and then they separate the babies from the rest of the herd and then try to sell them to zoos and circuses around the world."[8]

Finally, animal rights groups protest that the tricks and stunts circus animals are made to do are unnatural and inhumane. "In the wild, bears don't ride bicycles, tigers don't jump through fiery hoops, and elephants don't stand upright on their hind legs. Circuses portray a distorted view of wildlife," comments PETA.[9]

> • **At circuses and marine parks, animals are made to behave in ways that they never would in their natural environments. How important is it for an animal in captivity to be allowed to act as it would in the wild?**

Marine parks, where dolphins (including "killer whales," or orcas, which are a type of dolphin and not actually whales), whales, seals, sea lions, walruses, seabirds such as puffins and penguins, and other aquatic animals perform or go on display for large audiences, are just as cruel as circuses, say animal rights advocates. As with circuses, marine parks capture many of their animals in the wild. Cetaceans—whales, dolphins, and porpoises—are highly social creatures used to living in large family groups, or pods. When members of these pods are captured, it disrupts the entire social structure. "To obtain a female dolphin of breeding age, for example," according to PETA, "boats are used to chase the pod to shallow waters. The dolphins are surrounded with nets that are gradually closed and lifted into the boats. Unwanted dolphins are thrown back. Some die from the shock of their experience. Others slowly succumb to pneumonia caused by water entering their lungs through their blowholes. Pregnant females may spontaneously abort their babies." [10]

Once in an exhibit, cetaceans, which typically travel dozens of miles a day out in the open oceans, are restricted to an area of only a few dozen square yards—and with water between 24 and 35 feet deep. The lifespan of these animals is often shorter than it would be in the wild, according to PETA:

> In the wild, dolphins can live to be 25 to 50 years old. Male orcas live between 50 and 60 years, females between 80 and 90 years. But orcas at Sea World and other marine parks rarely survive more than 10 years in captivity. More than half of all dolphins die within the first two years of captivity; the remaining dolphins live an average of only six years. One Canadian research team found that captivity shortens an orca's life by as much as 43 years, and a dolphin's life by up to 15 years. [11]

In order to maintain good public relations, accuses Joan

Dunayer, marine parks try to hide the number of animals that die under their care:

> Because so many aquatic animals die prematurely in captivity, their captors conceal the toll in lives. Three days after the Scott Aquarium opened at the Henry Doorly Zoo (Omaha), all moon jellies (jellyfishes) in a tank died. The aquaprison posted this sign at the tank: "Animals temporarily off display." At Sea World different orcas perform under the same name (Shamu, Namu, or Baby Shamu); offstage, orcas such as Orky and Corky bear the same names as predecessors. . . . The practice presents a false picture of orca longevity. In its annual reports to the National Marine Fisheries Service, Sea World omits the personal names of nearly all its marine mammal captives, making it difficult for outsiders to know which of them have died.[12]

Because the longevity of these animals is severely truncated and their emotional and physical health compromised, according to animal rights organizations, marine parks are one target they aim at in the goal to restore freedoms to creatures that are, in many cases, highly intelligent and social beings.

Rodeos and racetracks exploit animals for sport and gambling.

While much of the abuse that takes place at zoos, circuses, and marine parks goes on behind the scenes, the poor treatment of animals is very public indeed at the popular American event called the rodeo. Although animals aren't killed outright, as they are in bullfighting, which is popular in countries such as Spain and Mexico, bull and bronco riding and cattle roping cause great distress to animals that even the most casual spectator can easily witness. Horses and bulls are choked with leather straps and shocked with electric prods to get them to jump and kick as the rider hangs on; young calves are chased down by a cowboy on horseback with a rope, lassoed, and then thrown to the ground and bound. Because it is patently clear that these animals are not by any stretch of the imagination having a good time, many activist groups believe rodeos should be outlawed. However, since this is not likely to happen any time soon, they instead campaign and ask individuals, businesses, and organizations to boycott rodeos.

> • **Rodeos and horseracing are cultural traditions in the United States with a long history. How do you think people would react if there were a ban on rodeos and races? Might people still take part in them illegally?**

With horse and dog races, it might appear as if the animals are enjoying the exercise of running around a track. In dog races, the canines—usually greyhounds—chase a fake rabbit around the track in what seems like a game for them; similarly, horse jockeys and trainers will often say that their horses eagerly participate in races. But, in addition to whipping horses with crops to make them run faster, there may be abuses that occur behind the scenes that may be damaging the animals' health. Much of this abuse involves surgeries that are performed on horses in order to make them race better. One such procedure is called "tubing." A tube is stuck into a hole in the horse's neck to send more oxygen to the bloodstream, which theoretically improves the horse's performance on the track. An old traditional therapy called "firing" involves actually burning the skin of a horse with an electric plate. The purpose of this is to inflame the area of an injury in a temporary treatment that is supposed to prolong a horse's ability to run and jump in the short term. Similarly, pin firing involves inserting a heated needle into a leg tendon. According to the British organization Animal Aid, "research suggests that this method can actually aggravate existing problems." [13]

Racehorses are subject to a variety of illnesses that would be less common in the wild, maintains Animal Aid, including increased heart rates, bleeding lungs, bone damage, and ulcerated stomachs. Rates for these afflictions range from between 55 percent to, in the case of ulcerated stomachs, 100 percent. To combat these ills, veterinarians hired by horse owners often inject the animals with painkillers. This doesn't cure the problem, but it does allow the horse to keep on racing. On top of this, racehorses suffer from psychological problems because they are bred to run but spend much of their time confined to stables. "Everything we have done to horses is unnatural to them," according to Margi Stickney, a lecturer on horse psychology. "Nothing we make them do relates to what they were meant to be, a continuously grazing, moving animal. . . . After horses come to racetracks, you see a change in their personalities. You've built this machine to perform, but you keep it restrained for most of the time. . . . We've essentially put them in jail." [14]

Because racehorses are very valuable to their owners (proven winners can be worth millions of dollars as breeding stock), it is important to maintain at least the more expensive horses in healthy condition. The same, say activists, is not necessarily true for greyhounds, which breed much more readily than horses. Greyhound racing, which is currently legal in only sixteen states in America, is infamous among animal rights and welfare groups. When dogs between the ages of two and five years were no longer fast enough to be raced, they were once routinely killed. However, since the 1980s, a variety of rescue organizations have sprouted up to save these animals. Groups such as the Greyhound Protection League and the Michigan Greyhound Connection take the dogs and adopt them out as pets.

Back in 1989, noted Susan Bilsky, president of the Michigan Greyhound Connection, about 46,000 greyhounds were killed because they were no longer useful in racing. That number went down to about 19,000 in 2000, thanks to rescue groups. That number, Bilsky says, is still too high, however, and includes more than 7,600 puppies deemed unworthy for racing. Greyhounds are typically bred at greyhound farms (sometimes called "puppy mills") and sold to tracks. Those that are used for racing receive a tattoo in one ear that indicates their racing number, and a tattoo in the other ear that indicates their birthdate. They are then raced until their performance level wanes. Because greyhound females typically have fifteen puppies in a litter, the dogs are easily replaced. For the same reason, these dogs do not get enough veterinary care. According to Bilsky, "It all depends on the racetrack owner, of course, and now that so much has come to light about these dogs some of them have cleaned up their act. It's not as bad as it used to be, but it can be bad. They are crated a lot of the time, and injuries go without any vet care. We know that the dogs are not inoculated in any way, no vaccines are given; that's even at the best of tracks." [15] To Bilsky, greyhound racing is simply a senseless sport that encourages abuse and needless death for thousands of animals. "We feel that dogs are exploited and used for nobody's benefit, really," she concluded. "Gambling is not anything anyone needs anyway." [16]

> • **What are your feelings about the way some dogs and cats are bred to enhance certain traits? Would you prefer to own a purebred pet that might have some inbred characteristics that could lead to future health problems, or a scruffy-looking mutt? How important are looks in a pet?**

Although in the past, humans did not know enough about science and species behavior to sufficiently care for the world's animals, today, people are capable of putting a stop to traditional exploitation of animals in entertainment venues, such as zoos and circuses. Like humans, animals desire to live freely in their own natural habitats and should not be taken from their homes to bring human beings pleasure or profit.

No Harm Is Done When Animals Are Used for Entertainment

Human beings have had a close relationship with animals over the centuries. That connection includes not only using animals for food, clothing, and labor, but also as a source of wonder, inspiration, and companionship. There is something within most people that finds other species fascinating and even lovable. Animals inspire artists to compose books, poems, and music; they give us comfort, and, according to some physicians, they even provide health and psychological benefits. Because of our attraction to animals, people often express a desire to see them firsthand. As our world becomes increasingly urbanized and overpopulated, however, and as habitats continue to be destroyed at an alarming rate, the prospects of seeing unusual animals in the wild becomes dim. Consequently, tourists flock to zoos, circuses, and marine parks for the chance to see elephants, tigers, and other exotic creatures. For most other people, owning a pet such as a dog or cat affords the contact with animals that we so often desire.

> • **How important is it for people to see exotic species of wildlife at zoos? Is it sufficient for us to watch nature programs on television, or is there something important about seeing such creatures live?**

Zoos, circuses, and marine parks, like research laboratories, are subject to the Animal Welfare Act, as well as other federal regulations, such as the Endangered Species Act and the Convention on International Trade in Endangered Species (CITES). Local and state governments often have their own laws that must be followed as well. Circuses face inspections by the U.S. Department of Agriculture, and zoos are also inspected by the American Zoo and Aquarium Association (AZA). Should the AZA refuse to accredit a zoo because of a failure to meet guidelines regarding the health and safety of the animals, the zoo will be denied the right to obtain and house exotic and endangered species. Despite these regulations, which are designed to ensure the safety and health of both wildlife and the public, PETA and other animal rights groups typically question the wisdom of having domestic and wild species put on public display or even used for companionship. The question then becomes whether it is realistic, in our ever-shrinking world, to expect that we can sever all contact with other species on the planet.

Zoos are a work in progress.

Zoos were once nothing more than entertainment venues where people could go and look at exotic species, sometimes even seeing them put on wildlife acts. In recent decades, that has changed considerably. Zoos are now playing an increasing role in the effort to preserve vanishing wildlife. For the most part, animals are no longer captured in the wild, but are instead bred at zoos, which exchange them through the Species Survival Plan (SSP) for breeding purposes. Exhibits are being constructed to closely simulate natural surroundings, so that animals are more comfortable. Some zoos have even become facilities for scientific research so that biologists can better understand different species' needs. This, in turn, helps conservationists decide which remaining habitats are most critical to set aside for wildlife reserves, and also help zookeepers and curators provide better care for their animals.

> • **Now that their habitat is disappearing, is the only hope for wild animals to have some of their kind living in zoos in order to maintain the population?**

Despite these efforts, animal rights activists describe zoos as animal prisons, complaining that they don't provide enough space, that the environment is artificial, and that animals are subjected to abuse. In response, Dr. Ron Kagan, director of the

Species Survival Plan

The Species Survival Plan began in 1981 as a cooperative population management and conservation program for selected species in zoos and aquariums in North America. Each SSP manages the breeding of a species in order to maintain a healthy and self-sustaining population that is both genetically diverse and demographically stable.

Beyond this, SSPs participate in a variety of other cooperative conservation activities, such as research, public education, reintroduction and field projects. Currently, 106 SSPs covering 161 individual species are administered by the American Zoo and Aquarium Association, whose membership includes accredited zoos and aquariums throughout North America.

Source: American Zoo and Aquarium Association. Available online at *http://www.aza.org/ ConScience/ConScienceSSPFact/*.

Detroit Zoological Institute and Society, admits that zoos are not perfect, but these days, they are being designed more and more to benefit animals and to change public attitudes toward wildlife and the environment. As he states:

> There's a qualified defense of zoos in that sense. A great zoo . . . potentially can have an impact in terms of helping wildlife. But I think some of the traditional stated objectives of zoos and aquariums as they relate to conservation may be or not all that defensible. Clearly, just as the Nature Conservancy will never be able to buy enough land to really protect nature, zoos will never be able to save enough individual animals to be able to save species. So I think it's important to not overstate what zoos and aquariums can do. In terms of what they can do, obviously the issue of direct conservation work either in the field or in captivity is one element of it. There's a limited amount, but certainly significant things can and have been done. But secondarily, clearly the biggest potential impact is an indirect one through our direct connection with the public and interaction with often millions of visitors.[1]

Responding to those who say that animals are sometimes harmed at zoos, Kagan states frankly that sometimes abuse has occurred, but the fault is not inherent in zoos. Rather, the blame should be placed with individual people:

> Zoos don't abuse animals, people abuse animals. There have been people who have worked in zoos who have abused animals, and there are people in the rest of society that have abused animals. As PETA is fond of quoting me, anytime anyone physically abuses or hits an animal, in my view they should be prosecuted for cruelty, and it doesn't matter whether it's somebody in a zoo or somebody on the street. [2]

- **At zoos, keepers often try to come up with toys and other "enrichment items" for the animals to explore so that they don't become bored. Couldn't the performance routines that circus animals go through also be considered "enrichment" activities?**

Speaking about Alan Green's book *Animal Underworld,* in which the author documents cases where zoo animals were sold to unscrupulous dealers, Kagan is blunt:

> I think we know that historically some of it *was* true, and I think the profession has a lot to answer for. Part of it, I think, was reckless, part of it was just irresponsible people weren't really paying attention, people weren't doing their job in a very meticulous way, and I think part of it [was] that there are people in this world who think that animals are commodities, and so they're bought and sold so what's the difference? That, to me, is very alarming. I don't think there are many people like that in the zoo community, and I think every day there are fewer and fewer, but I'm sure that some of what is in that book is accurate.[3]

But does this mean that zoos can't justify their existence? Should we close down zoos around the country and around the world because of errors that were made in the past? Kagan, an indisputable realist about the present state of wildlife in the world and the role zoos play in it, thinks not. The condition of zoos in the United States is not ideal, but he feels we are finally beginning to learn what zoos *should* be in the future. In fact, he teaches a course on the subject at Michigan State University. According to Kagan, if zoos of the future are less concerned about trying to exhibit only the types of animals that people want to see and instead restructure themselves with the main goal of preserving animals species and changing people's attitudes about them, then there may be hope:

The problem is that in the old days the decisions were simply, well we want to see this type of monkey or that type of cat, or a curator likes that type of animal and that's why an institution would have them. More and more there's a lot more analysis to what we can deliver, whether we've got a decent climate for the type of animal, whether we have enough space, if we've got the right types of expertise. There are a lot of considerations, and I think more and more of them are playing out, and I think generally what we ought to be seeing is less is more. In other words, we ought to be seeing more and more zoos with fewer animals because they're giving much more space to different types of animals. Not all need lots of space, but many do; and more resources are given, and so you're focusing more on quality than quantity, and that, I think, is a very positive thing.[4]

With the present political, social, and economic state of the world, in Kagan's opinion, zoos will be unable to save the world's wildlife. However, that doesn't mean things won't change in the future and that zoos should not make the effort. Some zoos today are involved in initiatives to reintroduce animals to the wild, and some limited success has been made, including the reintroduction of Arabian oryxes, golden lion tamarin monkeys, Przewalski's horses, black-footed ferrets, and California condors, among others. Some institutions, such as the Cincinnati Zoo, now have what are called "frozen zoos," facilities that cryogenically freeze the embryos and sperm of various endangered species (freezing eggs so far has met with only very limited success) in the hope that they may be used to produce young in the future. If no female animals from a species are available to be impregnated, sometimes other suitable species may be used for gestation. For instance, at Cincinnati, an antelope species called the eland was impregnated with the embryo of a rare bongo and successfully gave birth to a bongo calf. Problems with this method, however, include the fact that some animals need to acquire learned behaviors from their parents and may not have that opportunity available to them.

But without enough habitat for these animals to live in, such efforts are ultimately doomed to failure unless something in people's attitudes can be changed. Perhaps this is the most important role zoos can play. Says Kagan:

> I think we have to put our focus on helping to shape constructive values in society. Zoos really have always been about people at least as much as they've been about animals. Zoos should take on a role of understanding that the real mission is shaping attitudes about nature and about animals. That is done in part through the interaction with animals, and also that interaction is being redefined as we go along. It used to be shows and now it isn't. There are other ways to interact which are not harmful to animals. I do think, though, that the biggest opportunity and the most important thing we can be doing deals more with the interface with the public and the interpretation of nature and the interpretation of what's going on between us and nature, and ultimately offering people some viable and reasonable, not fanatical, but reasonable strategies that they can live their lives to not damage nature but rather help it.[5]

In the meantime, zoos will do all they can to keep our remaining species from becoming extinct. "There is a place [for zoos]," concludes Kagan, "but that place would look different than it does today. It would have nowhere near as many animals. It would have things like we do [at the Detroit Zoo], like simulators and other things so that there are certain things that can be accomplished that don't require live animals. A lot of theater, a lot of innovative, different types of interpretive tools; the use of art, things like that. I'm hoping that the zoo at the end of the century looks very little like the zoo of the last century."[6]

Circuses and marine parks can serve valuable purposes.

More people are aware these days that zoos are involved in wildlife conservation, but some might be surprised that marine parks and circuses are also getting into the act of educating the public and researching ways to protect endangered species. SeaWorld/Busch Gardens, for example, runs a conservation fund that partners with organizations around the world to help protect aquatic species such as penguins, right whales, dolphins, otters, seabirds, sea turtles, and sharks, as well as terrestrial species, including African elephants, rhinos, tigers, cheetahs, gorillas, orangutans, lions, hyenas, and hippopotami. Marine parks are important, too, in helping the public learn more about marine wildlife. As Fred Jacobs, senior director of communications at Busch Gardens Entertainment Corporation, insists, "I don't think anyone would argue that visitors to a SeaWorld park leave with a keener appreciation and respect for the animals they have seen and a much greater likelihood to preserve and protect them in the wild. There is no question that a greater understanding and empathy for these animals exists today than a generation ago."[7]

> • **If you have ever visited a circus, marine park, or zoo, has this changed your attitude about animals in any way? If so, how?**

Animal rights activists, as well as many other people, such as Detroit Zoo director Ron Kagan, believe it is impossible to provide a large cetacean with enough room in captivity. Jacobs, however, refutes that notion:

> People who make this claim invariably have no scientific support for it. Our habitats for whales and dolphins are the largest man-made bodies of saltwater ever constructed. Our killer whale pools contain nearly seven million gallons of continually filtered and chilled seawater. The U.S. government has established minimum standards for the size of marine

mammal habitats and SeaWorld pools meet or exceed them in every case. These standards are based on sound scientific principles. We also house whales and dolphins with other members of their species, give them regular veterinary examinations and treatment, exercise and mental stimulation. As a result, the health of our animals is exceptionally good, as is our record of breeding success.[8]

The issue of training these animals is similar to what goes on in circuses. Jacobs points out that abuse is not only intolerable but unwise. "You do not abuse an animal that is capable of tearing a bull sea lion in half and then enter the water with it," he notes wryly. Training and performances are stimulating for the marine animals, he maintains, and therefore beneficial:

> There are two ways to think about this. First, what is the effect on the animals and, second, what is the effect on the humans watching? For the animal, a trained behavior is the result of a long and stimulating process. Training at SeaWorld is based entirely on positive reinforcement so a trusting relationship between animal and trainer is essential. Then consider that each animal will know anywhere from a few dozen to more than 100 discrete behaviors and you get a sense of the depth of that bond. For visitors, the effect can be just as profound. Many of the people who work as SeaWorld educators, trainers, biologists, and veterinarians today were inspired by things they saw at SeaWorld as children.[9]

Some circuses, too, are very involved in conservation. For example, Ringling Brothers and Barnum & Bailey Circuses has invested over $5 million to build the Center for Elephant Conservation. Located in Florida, the facility is designed to help preserve Asian elephants, whose numbers have declined in recent years to fewer than 40,000 individuals in the wild. Because of efforts like these, Barbara Pflughaupt, national representative for Ringling Brothers, bristles when asked about PETA's charges of animal cruelty at circuses:

> I can't speak for any other circuses, and wouldn't, but I can speak for ours. We raise some of our own animals; we might contract with individuals who have animals to come over with a one or two year tour with their animals. The animals we own and we keep and manage and take care of, are elephants, horses, camels, and we buy them either from dealers here, people that raise them, or we raise them ourselves. In terms of elephants, what's important to note and what the critics of circuses will tell you, quite frankly, is that we pull them from the wild, we rip babies from their mothers. That is completely incorrect and misinformation. At Ringling Brothers we follow the CITES treaty that the United States is a part of, and in the early 1970s CITES determined that taking Asian elephants out of the wild was not something people can do and we have not done that and we do not do that.[10]

PETA has also publicized films that allegedly show elephants and other animals being harmed with bullhooks or struck with pipes and whips. Such abusive practices are categorically denied by Pflughaupt, who comments that such film clips are years out of date, are shown out of context, or weren't filmed at the circuses that PETA claims they were. "[Animal abuse is] intolerable at Ringling Brothers," she says. "Any kind of mistreatment of our animals is against every policy that we have. It is not something that we can condone in any way, shape, or form, and we do not and we take immediate steps if there are any accusations to look into the issue and make sure that nothing is happening that is inappropriate."[11]

PETA has said that trainers at circuses strike and otherwise injure elephants, tigers, and other animals in order to make them submissive so that they are easier to train. Pflughaupt points out that negative reinforcement, as it is called, would not work in training an animal because instead of learning to do a trick, the animal instead would cower and cringe away from the trainer. "The way we train is with operant conditioning," she says, "and the basic rules of operant conditioning are that you reward positive behavior and you ignore negative behavior. Most animals and human beings will respond to reward for anything they do and they notice that if they're not getting rewarded for something they stop doing it." [12]

Indeed, she says, with humane treatment, elephants will not only perform better but will also look forward to show-time. "I believe they enjoy their interactions with human beings," says Pflughaupt. "They are very curious animals, and they seem to be as curious about me as I am about them. I have a lot of elephant friends. It's really true; I've spent 14 years around them. They are very special animals, very individual. Some are nicer than others, just like human beings. I believe they exhibit behaviors that indicate that there is pleasure involved in performing." [13]

> • **Which method do you believe would be more effective in training an elephant or tiger to obey commands: striking it with a whip or bullhook, or coaxing it with food rewards and affection?**

When circus animals aren't performing, they are housed in comfortable accommodations, says Ringling Brothers. "We pride ourselves on the level of care and the healthy environment we provide for all our animal performers," Ringling Brothers asserts on its Website. "In arenas where space permits, our animal facility is outdoors and in the full view of the public. Each animal is groomed daily. The entire stable area, as well as individual animal stalls, is kept clean around the clock. We often provide guided tours of our facility for animal experts and media." [14] Furthermore, when animals travel on tours, they ride in "custom-made traveling cars," are under constant care and supervision, and, on longer trips, are given regular rest stops.

Pflughaupt feels that PETA's attacks on circuses are motivated more by politics than by a genuine desire to see that animals are cared for:

> Quite frankly, most of our critics that harangue us the most are people whose agenda is to end the use of all animals in entertainment. It's not just about care. They spend none of their money on the care of animals. We spend a great deal of our money on the care of each and every animal we own. If you investigate where the money for animal rights groups goes—and you can because the federal government makes that available to the public—you'll see that 90 percent of their money goes to fundraising efforts and advertising and politically motivated campaigns. They don't give money to shelters; they don't save individual animals. Their lawsuits . . . take up the courts' time and money.
>
> It's . . . a political agenda. It's people who want to tell Americans what to eat and what to wear and how they can be allowed to spend their free time. If someone does not agree with the idea of animals and humans working together then they don't have to support it, but they should not be in a position to make that decision for everyone, nor should they be allowed to misinform and to manipulate facts in order to raise money from people. I also believe they should tell people their true agenda. There are organizations that are animal rights organizations that never tell you that if they have their way you would not own a horse because you would have to train it and house it; we could not have seeing eye dogs because they don't believe in training any animals for humans' use; you would not be able to have companion animals. If you look at [PETA president] Ingrid Newkirk, certainly her position is that she does not believe in companion animals either. Ultimately, she does

not believe you should have a dog or live with a cat. She believes you should only observe them from a distance. You shouldn't go whale watching because you destroy [the whales'] environment.[15]

Ultimately, asserts Pflughaupt, because of our shrinking world we will have to learn to coinhabit this planet or risk losing animals such as the elephant forever. Fortunately, in her mind, it is possible for people and animals to live together. She concludes:

We have to be aware that we are pushing species off the face of the Earth and they will not be able to survive without us. It is an ivory tower position to say that animals should be left out in the wild. They can't be and survive. . . . It won't be possible. I believe very strongly that good working relationships between animals and humans are the best way to save the planet and that any species that is going to survive will have to adapt to changing conditions. Asian elephants cannot live in their range states anymore, and there are experts that say within 40 years they will disappear, and there will only be elephants that are in captivity because we are willing to put in what it takes to take care of them.[16]

The harm caused by rodeos and racetracks is highly exaggerated.

Those who work with animals at various entertainment venues usually respond to animal rights activists' claims of abuse and misconduct by saying that the activists are misrepresenting the facts, and the racing and rodeo industries are no different. For example, according to the Greyhound Racing Association of America (GRAA), the Pennsylvania Citizens Against Greyhound Racing (PCAGR), an animal rights group, interpreted statistics released by the National Greyhound Association (NGA) in a way that made it look as if greyhound racing were responsible for the deaths of thousands of dogs between 1989 and 1998. During this period, the PCAGR estimates that 426,407 puppies were born but only 342,022 were registered by the time they were eighteen months old. However, says the GRAA, records on the number of litters whelped were not kept before 1995, so it is unclear where the PCAGR obtained its figures. Furthermore, the PCAGR estimates that 7,000 greyhound puppies "disappeared" in 1999 and that 20,000 adults were killed. This is based on the figure that 27,000 dogs exited the system, 12,000 of which were adopted. "Here," states the GRAA, "even the math is off. If 12,000 were adopted out of 27,000 they assume exited the racing system, that leaves 15,000. But they claim 7,000 disappeared and 20,000 were killed."[17]

The GRAA also complains that animal liberationists make other assumptions, do not cite actual printed reports, and distort information to suit their needs. "They have reviewed statistics and found ways to twist them to make their twisted point," says the GRAA. "Where they can't twist statistics they manufacture them. And most adoption groups will tell you the dogs they get from the tracks, farms and trainers are in good general health. There will always be exceptions, but abused, sick, and injured dogs are NOT the rule."[18] Greyhounds live in humane conditions and receive good care, insists the GRAA, and when their racing careers are done, they are typically adopted out.

A racing greyhound can cost an owner thousands of dollars, but horses are even more expensive. A champion racehorse can cost tens, even hundreds, of thousands of dollars. Some of the most valuable horses have sold for millions. Feeding, lodging, and providing veterinary care for a horse is pricey as well. Most horse owners love their animals and would not agree with accusations of abuse that the animal rightists aim at them. Even if they didn't have an emotional attachment to their horses, it would not make financial sense for those who own racehorses to harm them. The same is true for rodeo horses. Large animal veterinarian Dr. Susan McCartney backs this up when she notes: "It's really not economically feasible for these stock contractors [people who raise animals for rodeos] not to take good care of these animals, if for no other reason but their resale value."[19]

Accusations that horses, bulls, and calves are harmed at rodeos are also greatly exaggerated, according to the Professional Rodeo Cowboys Association (PRCA), which states:

> Professional rodeo's seven events are physically demanding and, therefore, certainly not free of risk. But neither are they as dangerous as rodeo's critics claim. A 1998–99 survey conducted at 19 PRCA rodeos indicated that the injury rate for animals was so low it was statistically negligible. Of the 27,767 animal exposures, just 15 were injured, according to the data compiled by on-site veterinarians. That translates to an injury rate of five-hundredths of 1 percent—.00054 to be exact.[20]

Although animals used in rodeos and horse and dog racing are not covered in the United States under the Animal Welfare Act, there are a variety of state and local regulations that do protect them. Furthermore, the transportation of animals is covered under the federal Twenty-Eight Hour Law of 1994, which states that animals must be allowed to rest periodically when being moved long distances. In some cases, national associations such as the PRCA also oversee standards of conduct that apply to all their members. Rodeo advocates assert that these regulations, along with the animal owners' personal care for and vested financial interest in their animals, are enough to make sure that sporting animals are treated well and are happy.

> • **Is it all right for organizations like the Professional Rodeo
> Cowboys Association and the Greyhound Racing Association
> of America to set their own standards of animal care, or
> should the government set strict regulations on rodeos
> and racing?**

Entertainment venues that feature animals provide a valuable
means of educating people about different species and helping
to preserve wildlife around the globe. In the modern world, the
lives of animals and humans are far too intertwined to allow for
a reasonable separation to take place.

The Debate Continues

I s modern science causing the Holocaust-like torture of animal species in laboratories, or is animal experimentation essential medical research that results in cures for deadly diseases? Is the meat industry a money-grubbing business that entails the barbaric confinement and slaughter of innocent livestock for profit, or is it a humane and necessary agricultural process that feeds the world's hungry millions? Do those who work at zoos, circuses, and entertainment venues such as marine parks and rodeos simply want to use animals as a way of making money without regard to the creatures' welfare, or do they really care about the animals and want to do what is best for them? Both sides of these arguments appear to be based on genuine concern for the welfare of other species, but what the debate over animal rights really comes down to is one question: Is it in the best interest of the planet's animals to sever all ties with humanity or not?

Pro – Animal Rights Campaigns and Attitudes

Animal rights, in the purest definition of the term, concludes that any animal involvement with people can only lead to the pain and suffering of nonhuman species. The human-animal relationship should therefore be put to an end. Organizations that follow this credo have slowly been gaining members over the last few decades. Vegetarianism, too, is on the rise. Andrew Butler of PETA has compared the members of his group to those who fought for the civil rights of African Americans in the 1950s and 1960s, believing this cause is just as important and involves the same issues of what is fair and right:

> If anyone takes the time to actually come to the building to see the work we do and find out the sort of people who work here, you'll see that by and large [these are] . . . people who care about social issues across the board. Many of the people here come from the environmental movement, they come from the human rights movement, they come from areas such as helping in soup kitchens and helping with homeless projects in their areas. These are people who just care deeply about equality; they fight against prejudice and oppression wherever it occurs. This is an area—animal rights—which really has a great deal of crossover to many of these other areas. What we do to animals generally has a very negative and direct effect on the environment, on our health, and a whole range of other issues.[1]

As part of its attempt to break ties between humans and other species, PETA has resorted to various media-drawing tactics in order to gain public attention for its cause. For example, to protest circuses, PETA has organized the "Crouching Tiger, Hidden Cruelty" campaign, in which naked women are painted to look like tigers and displayed in public before a circus comes to town in order to protest what the group considers cruelty in circuses. PETA members have also dumped huge piles

Striving to Reduce the Sum Total of Suffering After 9/11

by Ingrid Newkirk

People for the Ethical Treatment of Animals' staff members were on the streets of Manhattan soon after the attack on the World Trade Center. We arrived with fully equipped rescue vans, introduced ourselves to the emergency personnel guarding Ground Zero, and went to work helping reunite bereaved and shell-shocked people with frightened animals locked without food or water in structurally unsound blocks of apartments in the "hot zone." Eight days after the attack, we were still getting exhausted, dehydrated animals into waiting human arms.

Perhaps that's one reason why it was so hideous to us that columnist Andy MacFarlane accused [PETA] of being supporters of terrorism. PETA does not condone or commit violent acts, nor do we threaten anybody with violence—even those who make their livings committing violence against animals. Our whole reason to exist is to combat violence to innocents: in the slaughterhouse, the laboratory, on the fur farm, and behind the Big Top, among other places. The accusation is an affront to us and to the victims of real terrorism in New York City and elsewhere.

You could call us "terra-ists." We value animal life, and more. We strive to reduce the sum total of suffering, not only to people but to all other species, and the earth. We oppose violence in the broadest sense, not in some mean, narrow definition of it that excludes everyone who doesn't walk on two legs. We think eating non-violently and behaving non-violently to animals benefits humans, spiritually and physically.

Our goal is purely peaceful—we ask people to stop treating animals (and each other) like objects without feelings. The most "violent" thing we've ever done was to lob a bit of tofu "cream" pie, vaudeville style, at a clothing designer who still uses animal skins. We are devoted to getting ordinary people to help make a difference, legally and peacefully, for the animals who cannot defend themselves. We work every day to provide options to students and housewives, to people in of manure outside agricultural shows and have published provocative ads, such as one in which cheerleader and actress Bonnie-Jill Laflin poses topless on a pile of hay, to protest rodeos.

business and to shoppers. We also work with government agencies and law enforcement to see that animal protection laws are enforced. We help people understand that the choices we make—what cosmetics we buy, what we eat for dinner, what we wear and what amusements we choose—can either help or hurt animals.

So much of what is done to animals occurs out of sight. Most people never know about it until some brave soul blows the whistle, often by calling PETA. Once we know where and how animals are suffering, we do whatever we can—within the bounds of the law—to draw attention to the abuse and stop it. A few examples: At a pig breeding farm, workers mercilessly beat and kicked pigs, and even butchered them alive; at General Motors, pigs were strapped into restraint devices and their heads were pummeled with powerful hydraulic devices; in one research laboratory, a "technician" beat rabbits to death with his fists; at another, experimenters sliced the toes off guinea pigs as a crude means of identification; at a university, dogs covered with painful sores were left untreated to die in their cages; on a fur farm, minks were killed with injections of weed killer.

Of course, this is just the tip of the iceberg, but we did stop these atrocities, and many more. They were stopped, not by terrorism, but because PETA filed complaints with authorities, went to court or raised enough of a fuss that they ended. Even McDonald's, Burger King and Wendy's have agreed, following PETA's campaign, to allow laying hens and sows more space, and to pay unannounced visits to their slaughterhouses. We'd rather these places served only veggie burgers, and that's all we ask people to buy but, for the animals, any misery ended is a help.

Each of us has the power to make simple changes in our lives so that we don't support these cruelties. Sharing this peaceful message is PETA's mission.

Source: Available online at *http://www.ingridnewkirk.com/i-essay911.html*.

The caption next to Laflin reads: "Nobody Likes an Eight-Second Ride." The deliberately disgusting "Milk Sucks" campaign, showing children afflicted with excess phlegm, pimples, flatulence, and obesity, protests the dairy industry and asserts that milk, contrary to the "Milk Does a Body Good" ads placed by dairy producers, is actually harmful to people's health. Such campaigns, says Butler, "are very very measured and restrained responses in the face of the enormous suffering and the enormous abuse that we're combating." [2]

> • **Do you believe that some of the promotional activities that PETA has been involved in are too extreme, or are stunts such as naked tiger women necessary for animal rights groups to draw attention to their cause?**

The more radical Animal Liberation Front (ALF) has pursued tactics that some, including the FBI, have labeled terrorist acts, including burning or otherwise vandalizing buildings where animal research has taken place, destroying scientific equipment, and raiding scientific laboratories and fur farms to "liberate" the animal occupants. Members have also caused destruction to homes, automobiles, and businesses in protest against such issues as suburban sprawl and low-fuel economy SUVs. ALF is not a formally organized group. Its members include anyone who has conducted a raid against an animal research or agricultural facility and announced in some way that the act was committed on behalf of ALF. In the past, ALF has provided videotapes to PETA showing animal cruelty. PETA, however, denies having any formal affiliation with ALF or the similar "terrorist" group known as the Earth Liberation Front (ELF). Says Butler:

> This is stemming from those who seek to undermine the good work that we do, those who seek to continue to profit from animal exploitation. In the early years of PETA there were certainly instances where tapes and packages would arrive on

our doorstep, and these packages . . . contained documents and photographs and video footage taken from raids on laboratories. In those instances we publicized simply what was left on our doorstep, and I don't think that anyone could deny that those sorts of things were actually instrumental in exposing what went on behind the scenes in animal testing laboratories. There were some very high profile cases which led to PETA campaigns which were really groundbreaking, such as exposing the crash tests that GM was taking part in and getting those stopped. So there was that in the past, but I think most people don't have a good grasp or understanding of what these groups are. They are, by and large, autonomous organizations; they have no real structural leadership.[3]

- **Would you define the Animal Liberation Front as a terrorist group? What are the goals of a terrorist organization, and would ALF meet these conditions? Should the FBI treat ALF the same way it would a group like Al Qaeda?**

This is not to say, though, that PETA has not found what ALF has accomplished useful. According to PETA, ALF is a non-violent group that conducts its raids not to cause harm but to do what it can to save abused animals:

[ALF] breaks inanimate objects such as stereotaxic devices and decapitators in order to save lives. It burns empty buildings in which animals are tortured and killed. ALF "raids" have given us proof of horrific cruelty that would not have been discovered or believed otherwise. They have resulted in officials' filing of criminal charges against laboratories, citing of experimenters for violations of the Animal Welfare Act, and, in some cases, shutting down of abusive labs for good. Often ALF raids have been followed by widespread scientific condemnation of the practices occurring in the targeted labs.[4]

In the final estimation of animal rights groups, human exploitation of animals is a matter of people's selfishness. Our desires for food extracted from animals, research techniques that use animals to develop or improve medical treatments, and entertainment choices that make use of other species are frivolous, say activists, when compared with the basic and more important rights of animals to life and liberty. Alternatives to all of these practices, say animal liberationists, are available to us and are, indeed, healthier for people and the environment. As Peter Singer concludes in his book *Animal Liberation,* our continuing practices of animal exploitation are based on antiquated concepts that no longer apply to our modern world:

> The attitudes toward animals of previous generations are no longer convincing because they draw on presuppositions—religious, moral, metaphysical—that are now obsolete. . . . If, then, we can see that past generations accepted as right and natural attitudes that we recognize as ideological camouflages for self-serving practices; and if, at the same time, it cannot be denied that we continue to use animals to further our own minor interests in violation of their major interests, we may be persuaded to take a more skeptical view of those justifications of our own practices that we ourselves have taken to be right and natural.[5]

Those who support animal rights but might find the tactics of ALF and PETA too extreme have begun to gravitate toward a new movement whose attitude lies somewhere between animal liberation and animal welfare. "New welfarism," as it has been labeled by Gary L. Francione, is the idea that while animal rights should be the end goal, the present and ongoing aim is to make strides forward in animal welfare in the hope that this will eventually lead to a full liberation of animals in the future. Even though the new welfarists hold the same fundamental beliefs as PETA and ALF, their methods more closely resemble those of animal welfare organizations like the Humane Society.

A Final Counterargument

Debaters on the other side of the animal rights argument typically characterize those in favor of animal liberation as unrealistic idealists who often skew facts to suit their own political agenda or use unscrupulous tactics to gain adherents to their cause. Animal rights groups, they say, actively lie and mislead the public about what is really going on in research labs, farms, and entertainment venues in order to win supporters and funding. Should their agenda be carried out to its fruition, say some, the end result would be detrimental to human beings. As Frankie Trull of the Foundation for Biomedical Research concludes:

> I don't really sympathize with animal rights because the way they operate is they have their opinion and if you don't have their opinion then they become very hostile and aggressive. And that's no way to address an issue. Improving the quality of life of these animals, that's animal welfare and that's our responsibility. And we completely, 100 percent endorse that. Animal rights [groups want] no animal research for any reason, which the animal rights groups say all the time: "Even if animal research meant a cure for AIDS we'd be against it." That's pretty drastic, I think.[6]

Furthermore, say critics of ALF in particular, actions such as releasing animals from labs and farms into the wild are not doing the animals any favors. Trull had some examples of these exploits in mind:

> [I'm reminded] of a story where an animal rights group broke into a research facility at the University of Minnesota and let all the pigeons go. . . . They were part of a post-doc study and the woman [researcher] had been working with these birds for four or five years; I mean, they were her family. So they let them lose and of course they all died because they grew up in the lab. I mean, that's the other thing. These animals view this as home. The animal rights people "liberate" them and they die. Another story—this happened some years ago in England at a big pharmaceutical company. The animal rights people came in through the skylights and let 90 beagles go. So of course they want to escape this laboratory and be liberated, so the beagles take off and it's like a big, grassy campus. Anyway, the beagles broke out at like four o'clock in the morning. . . . Well, at five o'clock in the afternoon, here they all come [back] because it's dinnertime![7]

> • **Which is better for a laboratory animal: to remain in a laboratory and be experimented on or to be suddenly released into the wild where it will likely die?**

In another example, animal liberationists have released hundreds of mink from fur farms in places like Michigan, Wisconsin, and England. According to one account published on the National Animal Interest Alliance Website, the release of mink into the countryside caused a great deal of environmental damage:

> Terrorists in England added thousands of mink to an environment already suffering from a large population of these North American natives. Many of the released mink

were killed on the roads; others, showing no fear of humans, attacked pets, killed birds in a sanctuary, and entered homes and other buildings. Angry British citizens armed themselves with air guns and clubs to protect themselves and their families from these voracious and curious predators.[8]

Some anti-PETA, anti-ALF groups have also accused animal liberationists of making patently misanthropic statements to the press. On one Website, AnimalScam.com, a quote from an issue of *USA Today* is cited in which ALF activist Vivien Smith says, "I would be overjoyed when the first scientist is killed by a liberation activist."[9]

More typically, however, the tactic used is dissimilation, according to those who oppose PETA and ALF's agendas. For example, Barbara Pflughaupt of Ringling Brothers notes that PETA once claimed that the retailer Sears withdrew commercial support for the circus because it became convinced that Ringling Brothers was mistreating animals. The truth, however, was that Sears stopped the advertising campaign simply because the contract between the two businesses had, after a mutually beneficial relationship, expired. As Sears community relations manager John P. Connolly stated in a letter to PETA, "PETA's news release has caused confusion among the media. By stating that Sears has 'pulled its sponsorship,' you are creating the misperception that Sears abruptly ended the sponsorship. This is not true, and quite honestly, is damaging PETA's credibility with the media."[10] Other claims by PETA that Ringling Brothers violated USDA and Animal Welfare Act laws and regulations have also been refuted by representatives of the USDA in letters to PETA.[11]

> • **How can a person be sure that film clips and other information about alleged animal abuses are accurate? When you hear an animal rights group protest alleged animal mistreatment, do you assume its members are telling the truth, or do you explore the issue deeper before making a decision?**

Circuses, rodeos, zoos, farmers, ranchers, scientists, and others who work daily with animals in their jobs say that they are, indeed, concerned about animal welfare and that their work not only benefits people but, especially through zoos and veterinary medicine, animals as well. The modern world, the argument goes, is very different from what it was a century or more ago, when there were more wild spaces for animals to live in freely. Today, habitat worldwide is succumbing to an ever-increasing human population that, as of 2003, includes more than 6 billion people. Many species will likely become extinct in the near future if human beings do not intervene because there will simply be no place for them to live. Other species, such as domesticated pets and farm animals, have been so carefully bred to suit their functions in human society for so many centuries that they simply could not function outside of our care. For these reasons, say those who are against the animal rights agenda, the complete disassociation of all animals from people is just not possible.

Letter from USDA telling PETA that Ringling Bros. did not violate the Animal Welfare Act

I am writing to allay your concerns expressed at numerous meetings with our attorneys about the media reports surrounding the death on January 24, 1998, of the juvenile Asian elephant known as "Kenny" and the complaint filed by the United States Department of Agriculture (USDA) in AWA Docket No. 98-20.

As you are aware, certain media reports stated incorrectly that USDA had charged Ringling Bros. and Barnum & Bailey Circus (Ringling Bros.) with a violation of the Animal Welfare Act that resulted in the death of "Kenny." Contrary to the published reports, the complaint filed in AWA Docket No. 98-20 did not allege that Ringling Bros. was responsible for or that its actions contributed to the death of "Kenny." Also, Ringling Bros. has never been adjudged to have violated the AWA or the Regulations and Standards issued thereafter.

Source: Available online at *http://www.feldentertainment.com/pr/pressroom.asp*.

• **What do you think life will be like for wild animals fifty years from now? How about a hundred years?**

Compromise and Changing Attitudes

The growth of the animal rights movement is a direct side effect of changing public attitudes that have been greatly influenced by evolving demographics in our country. Most Americans today live in urban or suburban communities, where they have little contact with wildlife or farms and, therefore, often rely on what they see on television, in newspapers, and on the Internet for their information about animal welfare and animal rights issues. Without direct interaction with animals, it is easy to develop misguided attitudes because, with the exception of our pets, we lack firsthand experience. There are two possible consequences of this: We may either become apathetic about how animals are treated (for example, seeing meat merely as something we pick up in the supermarket or elephants as beings created to entertain us at zoos and circuses) or, influenced by fairy tales and the talking cartoon animals to which we are exposed as we grow up, we may anthropomorphize too much.

The fact that people need to recognize is that although animals are not human beings, they are not commodities either. There can be no doubt that, overall, humans have had a profoundly negative impact on other species worldwide. The question still remains, however, whether we are willing to take full responsibility for this fact and, if we do, what exactly we will do about it.

The Debate Over Animal Rights

1 Class A dealers raise animals specifically for the purpose of selling them to researchers. Class B dealers buy their animals from other sources, such as pet stores or animal shelters, and then resell them to researchers.
2 Mark Grebner, "Ingham County Animal Shelter Policies: 'What We're Really Doing,'" *Lansing State Journal,* May 25, 2003, p. 11A.
3 Interview with Mike Severino, conducted by Kevin Hile on June 23, 2003.
4 Ibid.
5 Interview with Mary Stid, conducted by Kevin Hile, June 19, 2003.
6 Ibid.
7 Genesis 1:26.
8 Rod Preece and Lorna Chamberlain, *Animal Welfare and Human Values.* Waterloo, Canada: Wilfrid Laurier University Press, 1993, p. 39.
9 Tom Regan, *The Case for Animal Rights.* Berkeley, CA: University of California Press, 1983, p. 142.
10 "Frequently Asked Questions." Available online at *http://www.peta-online.org/ fp/faq.html* (July 27, 2003).

Point: Animals Are Worthy of Certain Rights

1 Peter Singer, *Animal Liberation: A New Ethics for Our Treatment of Animals.* New York: Avon Books, 1975, pp. xii–xiii.
2 "Chimps Should Be Part of Human Genus, Scientists Say," Associated Press, May 20, 2003.
3 Irene M. Pepperberg, "Referential Mapping: A Technique for Attaching Functional Significance to the Innovative Utterances of an African Grey Parrot (*Psittacus erithacus*)," 11 *Applied Psycholinguistics,* 22, 29 (1990).
4 "Koko's World." Available online at *http://www.koko.org/world/* (July 27, 2003).
5 Karen de Seve, "Animal Intelligence: How Brainy Are They? Scientists Are Learning How Animals Talk, Think, and Feel." *Science World,* 56:6 (November 26, 2001), p. 8.

6 Jeffrey Moussaieff Masson and Susan McCarthy, *When Elephants Weep: The Emotional Lives of Animals.* New York: Dell Publishing, 1995.
7 Jane Goodall and Phillip Berman, *Reason for Hope: A Spiritual Journey.* New York: Warner Books, 1999.
8 Masson and McCarthy, p. 95.
9 "Animal Consciousness," *Stanford Encyclopedia of Philosophy.* Available online at *http://plato.stanford.edu/ entries/consciousness-animal/* (July 5, 2003).
10 Clive Wynne, "Do Animals Think?" *Psychology Today,* 32:50 (November 1999).
11 Michael W. Fox, *Inhumane Society: The American Way of Exploiting Animals.* New York: St. Martin's Press, 1990.
12 Interview with Andrew Butler conducted by Kevin Hile on June 26, 2003.
13 Gary Kowalski, *The Souls of Animals.* Walpole, NH: Stillpoint Publishing, 1991.
14 Jeremy Bentham, *Introduction to the Principles of Morals and Legislation.* Oxford, England: Clarendon Press, 1907 (originally published 1780).

Counterpoint: Animals Are Not Worthy of Rights Like Those of Humans

1 Aristotle, *Politics,* Book 1, chapter 8. Available online at *http://classics.mit.edu/ Aristotle/politics.1.one.html.*
2 Immanuel Kant, *Lectures on Ethics,* trans. L. Infield, New York: Harper Torchbooks, 1963.
3 Tim Stafford, "Animal Lib," *Christianity Today,* June 18, 1990.
4 Michael Allen Fox, *The Case for Animal Experimentation: An Evolutionary and Ethical Perspective.* Berkeley, CA: University of California Press, 1986, p. 37.
5 Ibid., p. 38.
6 Ibid., pp. 38–39.
7 Ibid., p. 39.
8 Ibid.
9 Peter Jenkins, "Ask No Questions," *The Guardian,* July 10, 1973.
10 Richard Conniff, "Fuzzy-Wuzzy Thinking about Animal Rights," *Audubon,* November 1990, p. 121.

11 Stephen Budiansky, "The Animal Point of View," *Atlantic Unbound,* December 9, 1998.

12 D.G. Ritchie, *Natural Rights: A Criticism of Some Political and Ethical Conceptions.* London: George Allen & Unwin, 1952, p. 107.

13 Steven J. Bartlett, "Roots of Human Resistance to Animal Rights: Psychological and Conceptual Blocks." Available online at *http://www.animallaw.info/articles/arussbartlett2002.htm* (July 18, 2003).

14 Ibid.

15 *Lujan* v. *Defenders of Wildlife* (90-1424), 504 U.S. 555 (1992).

16 Joseph Lubinski, "Introduction to Animal Rights." Available online at *http://www.animallaw.info/articles/ddusjlibinski2002.htm* (July 18, 2003).

17 Ibid.

18 David R. Schmahmann and Lori J. Polacheck, "The Case against Rights for Animals," *B.S. Environmental Affairs Law Review.* 22:747, 751 (1995).

19 Edwin A. Locke, "Animal 'Rights' versus Man's Rights: Animal 'Rights' Activists Want to Sacrifice Man's Rights." Available online at *http://www.aynrand.org/medialink/animal.html.*

20 Interview with Frankie Trull conducted by Kevin Hile on July 15, 2003.

Point: Animals Should Not Be Used in Medical Research

1 Jordan Curnutt, *Animals and the Law: A Sourcebook.* Santa Barbara, CA: ABC-CLIO, 2001.

2 Ibid.

3 Interview with Crystal Spiegel conducted by Kevin Hile on July 14, 2003.

4 Curnutt, *Animals and the Law: A Sourcebook.*

5 Available online at *http://www.stopanimaltests.com/u-hpvqa.html.*

6 Alex Pacheco with Anna Francione, "The Silver Spring Monkeys," *In Defense of Animals,* ed. Peter Singer, New York: Basic Blackwell, Inc., 1985, p. 136.

7 *State* v. *Taub,* 11848-81 (1981), Maryland District Court unreported case.

8 *Taub* v. *State,* 43 A.2d 819 (Md. 1983).

9 Michael W. Fox, *Inhumane Society: The American Way of Exploiting Animals.* New York: St. Martin's Press, 1990, p. 59.

10 C. Ray Greek and Jean Swingle Greek, *Sacred Cows and Golden Geese.* New York: Continuum International Publishing Group, 2000.

11 Ibid., p. 60.

12 Ibid., p. 67.

13 Interview with Crystal Spiegel conducted by Kevin Hile on July 14, 2003.

14 Peter Singer, *Animal Liberation: A New Ethics for Our Treatment of Animals.* New York: Avon Books, 1975, p. 67.

15 Curnutt, *Animals and the Law: A Sourcebook.*

Counterpoint: Animals Serve a Useful Purpose in Medical Research

1 "The Development of a Polio Vaccine," The Biomedical Research Trust, Available online at *http://www.bret.org.uk/nec2.htm.*

2 Richard Malvin, "Animals Critical to Better Research: Activists Provide Distorted Picture of Research Results," *Lansing State Journal,* November 19, 2002, p. 11A.

3 Seriously Ill for Medical Research Website. Available online at *http://www.simr.org.uk/pages/nobel_survey.html.*

4 Ibid.

5 Interview with Frankie Trull conducted by Kevin Hile on July 15, 2003.

6 Incurably Ill for Animal Research, Issues and Answers. Available online at *http://www.iifar.org/issues.html.*

7 Michael Allen Fox, *The Case for Animal Experimentation: An Evolutionary and Ethical Perspective.* University of California Press, 1986, p. 33.

8 Ibid., p. 35.

9 Neal Miller, "Understanding Psychological Man: A State-of-the-Science Report," *Psychology Today* 16 (May 1982): 52.

10 Interview with Frankie Trull conducted by Kevin Hile on July 15, 2003.

11 Incurably Ill for Animal Research, Issues and Answers. Available online at *http://www.iifar.org/issues.html.*

12 Ibid.

13 Interview with Frankie Trull conducted by Kevin Hile on July 15, 2003.

14 Ibid.

15 *American Legal Defense Fund* v. *Espy,* 23 F.3d 496 (D.C. Cir. 1994).

16 Interview with Frankie Trull conducted by Kevin Hile on July 15, 2003.

17 "Alternatives," Fund for the Replacement of Animals in Medical Experiments. Available online at *http://www.frame.org.uk/ Alternat.htm* (July 2, 2003).

18 Ibid.

19 Robert J. White, "Antivivisection: The Reluctant Hydra," *American Scholar,* 40, 3 (Summer 1971).

Point: Animals Should Not Be Used for Food and Clothing

1 C. David Coats, *Old MacDonald's Factory Farm.* New York: Continuum, 1989.

2 Ibid.

3 Interview with Andrew Butler conducted by Kevin Hile on June 26, 2003.

4 Michael W. Fox, *Eating with Conscience: The Bioethics of Food.* Troutdale, OR: NewSage Press, 1997.

5 Ibid.

6 Interview with Andrew Butler conducted by Kevin Hile on June 26, 2003.

7 Fox, *Eating with Conscience: The Bioethics of Food.*

8 Ibid.

9 Mercy for Animals Website. Available online at *http://www.mercyforanimals.org/ pork.asp* (July 8, 2003).

10 Ibid.

11 Interview with Nathan Runkle conducted by Kevin Hile on July 7, 2003.

12 Daniel Cohen, *Animal Rights: A Handbook for Young Adults.* Brookfield, CT: Millbrook Press, 1993.

13 Interview with Andrew Butler conducted by Kevin Hile on June 26, 2003.

14 Alan Green, *Animal Underworld: Inside America's Black Market for Rare and Exotic Species.* New York: Public Affairs, 1999, pp. 163–164.

15 Cathy Liss, "Trapping and Poisoning," in *Animals and Their Legal Rights: A Survey of American Laws from 1641 to 1990,* 4th ed. Animal Welfare Institute, 1990.

16 Ibid.

17 *The Animal Rights Handbook: Everyday Ways to Save Animal Lives.* Los Angeles, CA: Living Planet Press, 1990.

18 Ibid.

19 Interview with Nathan Runkle conducted by Kevin Hile on July 7, 2003.

20 *The Animal Rights Handbook: Everyday Ways to Save Animal Lives.*

21 Bruce Friedrich, "Vegetarianism in a Nutshell." Available online at *http://www.goveg.com* (July 8, 2003).

Counterpoint: Animals Should Be Used for Food and Clothing

1 Craig B. Stanford, *The Hunting Apes: Meat Eating and the Origins of Human Behavior.* Princeton, NJ: Princeton University Press, 1999, p. 5.

2 Ibid., pp. 65–66.

3 Interview with Dan Murphy conducted by Kevin Hile on July 10, 2003.

4 Bernard E. Rollin, *Animal Rights and Human Morality.* New York: Prometheus Books, 1981.

5 Interview with Kay Johnson conducted by Kevin Hile on July 10, 2003.

6 Ibid.

7 Interview with Dan Murphy conducted by Kevin Hile on July 10, 2003.

8 Ibid.

9 Ibid.

10 Interview with Kay Johnson conducted by Kevin Hile on July 10, 2003.

11 David Petersen, *Heartsblood: Hunting, Spirituality, and Wildness in America.* Washington, D.C.: Island Press, 2000.

12 Mark Damian Duda, et al. *Wildlife and the American Mind.* Harrisonburg, VA: Responsive Management, 1998.

13 Aldo Leopold, *A Sand County Almanac, with Essays on Conservation from Round River.* New York: Oxford University Press, 1966.

14 "Conservation Activities." Available online at *http://www.rmef.org/conservation_ section.html* (July 14, 2003).

15 David Petersen, *Heartsblood: Hunting, Spirituality, and Wildness in America.* Washington, D.C.: Island Press, 2000.

16 "PETA Way Off Target: What Else Is New?" Available online at *http://www. scifirstforhunters.org/content/website/ media/peta* (July 14, 2003).

17 "Real Fur and the Environment." Available online at *http://www. furcommission.com/environ/index. html* (July 14, 2003).
18 Ibid.
19 "Fur Is Natural . . . and Environmentally Sound." Available online at *http://www. furcommission.com/resource/perspect98. htm* (July 14, 2003).
20 "The Food Guide Pyramid." Available online at *http://www.usda.gov/cnpp* (July 14, 2003).
21 Robert C. Atkins, *Dr. Atkins' New Diet Revolution.* Rev. ed. New York: Avon Books, 1999, p. 21.

Point: Animals Should Not Be Used for Entertainment

1 Joan Dunayer, *Animal Equality: Language and Liberation.* Derwood, MD: Ryce Publishing, 2001, p. 74.
2 Vicki Croke, *The Modern Ark, The Story of Zoos: Past, Present and Future.* New York: Scribner, 1997, pp. 32–33.
3 Michael W. Fox, *Inhumane Society: The American Way of Exploiting Animals.* New York: St. Martin's Press, 1990, p. 151.
4 Alan Green, *Animal Underworld: Inside America's Black Market for Rare and Exotic Species.* New York: Public Affairs, 1999, pp. 76–77.
5 Ibid., p. 77.
6 Ibid., p. 78.
7 "Circuses." Available online at *http://www.mercyforanimals.org/ circuses.asp* (July 9, 2003).
8 Interview with Andrew Butler conducted by Kevin Hile on June 26, 2003.
9 "Quick Facts." Available online at *http://www.circuses.com/qfacts.html* (July 9, 2003).
10 "Marine Mammal Parks—Chlorinated Prisons." Available online at *http://www. peta.org/mc/facts/fsent8.html* (July 9, 2003).
11 Ibid.
12 Joan Dunayer, *Animal Equality: Language and Liberation,* p. 97.
13 "Horse Racing Fact File: Welfare Problems." Available online at *http://www.animalaid.org.uk/racing/ factfile/* (July 9, 2003).

14 Margi Stickney, *The Observer,* July 27, 1997, as quoted online at *http://www. animalaid.org.uk.racing/factfile/.*
15 Interview with Susan Bilsky conducted by Kevin Hile on June 27, 2003.
16 Ibid.

Counterpoint: No Harm Is Done When Animals Are Used for Entertainment

1 Interview with Ron Kagan conducted by Kevin Hile on July 14, 2003.
2 Ibid.
3 Ibid.
4 Ibid.
5 Ibid.
6 Ibid.
7 Interview with Fred Jacobs conducted by Kevin Hile on July 15, 2003.
8 Ibid.
9 Ibid.
10 Interview with Barbara Pflughaupt conducted by Kevin Hile on June 20, 2003.
11 Ibid.
12 Ibid.
13 Ibid.
14 "Amazing Animals: Get the Answers." Available online at *http://www. ringling.com/animals/answer.aspx* (July 15, 2003).
15 Interview with Barbara Pflughaupt conducted by Kevin Hile on June 20, 2003.
16 Ibid.
17 "Greyt Lifestyle." Available online at *http://www.gra-america.org/ greytlifestyle.htm* (July 16, 2003).
18 Ibid.
19 "Animal Welfare." Available online at *http://www.prorodeo.com/Sport/ Animals/7.welfarePubs.html* (July 15, 2003).
20 Ibid.

The Debate Continues

1 Interview with Andrew Butler conducted by Kevin Hile on June 26, 2003.
2 Ibid.
3 Ibid.
4 "Frequently Asked Questions." Available online at *http://www.peta.org/fp/faq.html* (July 17, 2003).

5 Peter Singer, *Animal Liberation: A New Ethics for Our Treatment of Animals.* New York: Avon Books, 1975.

6 Interview with Frankie Trull conducted by Kevin Hile on July 15, 2003.

7 Ibid.

8 "Terrorists Release Mink, Destroy Records to Intimidate Fur Farmers and Retailers." Available online at *http://www.naiaonline.org/body/articles/ archives/furterr.htm* (July 17, 2003).

9 AnimalScam.com Home Page. Available online at *http://www.animalscam.com/ quotes.cfm* (July 17, 2003).

10 John P. Connolly, in a letter to PETA dated January 25, 1999. Available online at *http://www.feldentertainment. com/pr/pressroom.asp.*

11 "Press Room." Available online at *http://www.feldentertainment.com/pr/ pressroom.asp* (July 29, 2003).

General

Cothran, Helen, ed. *Animal Experimentation: Opposing Viewpoints.* Greenhaven Press, 2002.

Curnutt, Jordan. *Animals and the Law: A Sourcebook.* ABC-CLIO, 2001.

Day, Nancy. *Animal Experimentation: Cruelty or Science?* Rev. ed. Enslow Publishers, 2000.

Guither, Harold D. *Animal Rights: History and Scope of a Radical Social Movement.* Southern Illinois University Press, 1998.

Wand, Kelly, ed. *The Animal Rights Movement.* Greenhaven Press, 2003.

Williams, Jeanne. *Animal Rights and Welfare.* H. W. Wilson, 1991.

Woods, Geraldine. *Animal Experimentation and Testing: A Pro/Con Issue.* Enslow Publishers, 2002.

In Favor of Animal Rights
Books

Amory, Cleveland. *Man Kind? Our Incredible War on Wildlife.* Harper & Row, 1974.

Animals and Their Legal Rights: A Survey of American Laws from 1641 to 1990. 4th ed. Animal Welfare Institute, 1990.

Coats, C. David. *Old MacDonald's Factory Farm: The Myth of the Traditional Farm and the Shocking Truth about Animal Suffering in Today's Agribusiness.* Continuum, 1989.

Cohen, Daniel. *Animal Rights: A Handbook for Young Adults.* Millbrook Press, 1993.

Fox, Michael W. *Eating with Conscience: The Bioethics of Food.* NewSage Press, 1997.

———. *Inhumane Society: The American Way of Exploiting Animals.* St. Martin's, 1990.

Green, Alan. *Animal Underworld: Inside America's Black Market in Rare and Exotic Species.* PublicAffairs, 1999.

Greek, C. Ray, and Jean Swingle Greek. *Sacred Cows and Golden Geese: The Human Cost of Experiments on Animals.* Continuum, 2001.

Harrison, Ruth. *Animal Machines.* Vincent Stuart, 1964.

Kowalski, Gary. *The Souls of Animals.* Stillpoint Publishing, 1991.

Mason, Jim, and Peter Singer. *Animal Factories.* Crown, 1980.

Masson, Jeffrey Moussaieff, and Susan McCarthy. *When Elephants Weep: The Emotional Lives of Animals.* Dell Publishing, 1995.

Newkirk, Ingrid. *Free the Animals!* Noble, 1992.

Phelps, Norm. *The Dominion of Love: Animal Rights According to the Bible.* Lantern Books, 2002.

Regan, Tom. *The Case for Animal Rights.* University of California Press, 1983.

———, and Peter Singer, eds. *Animal Rights and Human Obligations.* Prentice-Hall, 1976.

Scully, Matthew. *Dominion: The Power of Man, the Suffering of Animals, and the Call to Mercy.* St. Martin's, 2002.

Singer, Peter. *Animal Liberation: A New Ethics for Our Treatment of Animals.* Avon Books, 1975.

Wise, Steven M. *Drawing the Line: Science and the Case for Animal Rights.* Perseus Publishing, 2002.

———. *Rattling the Cage: Toward Legal Rights for Animals.* Perseus Books, 2000.

Websites
American Anti-Vivisection Society
www.aavsonline.org
One of the oldest animal rights groups in the country, the AAVS focuses on eliminating the use of animals in laboratory research.

Animal Legal Defense Fund
www.aldf.org
A national organization of attorneys who fight for animal rights in the courtroom, often on a pro-bono basis.

Animal Liberation Front

www.animalliberationfront.com

A group of loosely organized citizens who actively release animals from laboratories and farms and often commit acts of vandalism against people they feel support injustices against animals. The FBI considers ALF a domestic terrorist group.

AnimalsVoice.com

www.animalsvoice.com

An online resource for animal rights groups, this site was created by the publishers of *Animals Voice* magazine and includes a rich database of articles, images, interviews, and profiles concerning animal rights issues.

Animal Welfare Institute

www.awionline.org

An animal rights group founded in 1951 that fights against inhumane transport and the use of animals in research, farms, and hunting, among other causes.

Fund for Animals

www.fund.org

Founded by author Cleveland Amory in 1967, the Fund for Animals' motto is "We speak for those who can't." The main focus of this organization is to fight against hunting practices nationwide, but it is also an advocacy group for domestic animals.

Hunt Saboteurs Association

hsa.enviroweb.org/hsa.shtml

This British-based organization actively goes out into the field to deliberately spoil and frustrate hunters who are in pursuit of animals.

International Vegetarian Union

www.ivu.org

An international organization founded in 1908 that promotes vegetarianism.

League Against Cruel Sports

www.league.uk.com

A British organization opposed to hunting, especially hunting with the use of dogs.

Mercy for Animals

www.mercyforanimals.org
An Ohio animal rights group fighting against the use of animals in research, farms, circuses, rodeos, and more.

National Anti-Vivisection Alliance

www.navs.org
Another organization similar to the AAVS that fights against the use of animals in medical research, product testing, and education.

People for the Ethical Treatment of Animals

www.peta.org
Probably the most prominent animal rights group in the United States today, PETA raises funds for all types of pro–animal rights causes and runs numerous—sometimes controversial—media campaigns.

United Poultry Concerns

www.upc-online.org
The UPC is solely concerned with the way people treat chickens, turkeys, and other domesticated fowl in agriculture, science, education, and entertainment.

Against Animal Rights
Books

Arnold, Ron. *EcoTerror: The Violent Agenda to Save Nature: The World of the Unabomber.* Free Enterprise Press, 1997.

Fox, Michael Allen. *The Case for Animal Experimentation: An Evolutionary and Ethical Perspective.* University of California Press, 1986.

Gluck, John P., Tony DiPasquale, and F. Barbara Orlans. *Applied Ethics in Animal Research: Philosophy, Regulation, and Laboratory Applications.* Purdue University Press, 2002.

Leahy, Michael P. T. *Against Liberation: Putting Animals in Perspective.* Routledge, 1991.

Orlans, F. Barbara. *The Human Use of Animals: Case Studies in Ethical Choice.* Oxford University Press, 1998.

———. *In the Name of Science: Issues in Responsible Animal Experimentation.* Oxford University Press, 1993.

Peterson, David. *Heartsblood: Hunting, Spirituality, and Wildness in America.* Island Press, 2000.

Stanford, Craig B. *The Hunting Apes: Meat Eating and the Origins of Human Behavior.* Princeton University Press, 1999.

————, and Henry T. Bunn, eds. *Meat Eating and Human Evolution.* Oxford University Press, 2001.

Websites

American Meat Institute

www.meatami.com

A national organization of meat and poultry companies that educates its members about safe handling procedures and government legislation, protecting members' interests and promoting their products at home and abroad.

Americans for Medical Progress

www.amprogress.org

A nonprofit organization whose goal is to educate the public about the importance of animal testing in medical research.

Animal Agriculture Alliance

www.animalagalliance.org

Created to replace the now-defunct Animal Industry Foundation, the AAA works to educate the public about the farm industry and build support for farmers and ranchers.

AnimalRights.net

www.animalrights.net

A discussion group and site for resources offering information for the argument against animal rights groups.

AnimalScam.com

www.animalscam.com

Part of the Center for Consumer Freedom, this site was created specifically to debunk the claims of PETA and other animal rights groups.

Biomedical Research Education Trust

www.bret.org.uk

A British organization that provides speakers for secondary schools on the subject of the benefits of animal research.

Center for Consumer Freedom

www.ConsumerFreedom.com

Supported by food companies and restaurants, this nonprofit group fights for the rights of people to eat and drink whatever they wish.

Delta Society

www.deltasociety.org

This pro–animal welfare site promotes the health benefits of the human-animal bond through pet ownership.

Foundation for Biomedical Research

www.fbresearch.org

Founded in 1981, this organization promotes and supports the use of animals in scientific research, believing it will help both people and animals.

Fund for the Replacement of Animals in Medical Experiments (FRAME)

www.FRAME.org.uk

FRAME advocates the reduction of animals used in laboratories wherever possible, but recognizes that some animal research is still necessary to advance science.

Fur Commission USA

www.furcommission.com

This is an organization of mink farmers who work together to promote their industry and its benefits.

Incurably Ill for Animal Research

www.iifar.org

A national organization that promotes the benefits of using animals in research, testing, and education.

National Animal Interest Alliance

naiaonline.org

An organization of various business and scientific interest groups that promotes humane practices in using animals for food, clothing, research, and companionship.

The Official Site of Ted Nugent

www.tnugent.com

Rock star and Michigan native Ted Nugent has been a longtime advocate of hunting. This site includes many of his views about hunting.

Research Development Society

www.rds-online.org.uk

A British nonprofit organization dedicated to promoting the benefits of animal research in medicine.

Safari Club International

www.scifirstforhunters.org

Promotes the benefits of hunting in our society and lobbies against government regulations that would restrict hunting rights.

Seriously Ill for Medical Research

www.simr.org.uk

A British organization promoting the importance of using animals in medical research and emphasizing the patients' perspective on the issue.

Legislation and Case Law

Food, Drug and Cosmetic Act of 1938, 16 U.S.C. §§ 301-392

This broad piece of legislation includes many requirements and prohibitions intended to improve the safety of manufactured drugs. Included in this legislation is a provision that all pharmaceuticals must be tested on animals as part of the Food and Drug Administration approval process.

Animal Welfare Act of 1970, 7 U.S.C. §§ 2131-2157

Originally set up as the Laboratory Animal Welfare Act of 1966, the AWA set minimum standards for laboratories and animal dealers for the care and transport of dogs, cats, primates, rabbits, guinea pigs, and hamsters, and it required these facilities to be licensed. Coverage expanded to all "warm-blooded" animals in 1970, and the 1970 changes also required anesthetics, analgesics, and tranquilizers to be used whenever possible during an experiment. The 1970 changes also covered animals in pet stores and in exhibits, such as zoos. Amended again in 1972 by the secretary of agriculture, rats, mice, and birds in laboratories, as well as farm animals, horses, and animals exhibited at fairs and used in rodeos were specifically excluded from protection under the AWA. Because farm animals are excluded, it is permissible under the AWA for scientists to use farm animals for experiments in any way they choose without violating the act. Changes made in 1976 stated that research laboratories were subject to immediate fines—rather than being warned with a cease and desist order first—for any violations to the AWA. In 1990, an amendment was added that required shelters to hold animals for a minimum of five days before selling them to research facilities. Most recently, in 2002, an amendment was added under the Farm Bill that permanently excluded birds, mice, and rats from being included under the AWA's protections.

Sierra Club* v. *Morton, 405 U.S. 727 (1972)

Although this case did not directly involve animals it helped define what legal standing for other species might mean. The Sierra Club sued Secretary of the Interior Rogers Morton for allowing development on land that was supposed to be protected as national forest. The suit was rejected because the Sierra Club failed to prove it had legal standing as a party that would be injured in some way by the development project. However, in a dissenting opinion, Justice William O. Douglas stated that natural objects, such as forestlands, could be considered to have legal standing as things that could be injured.

Endangered Species Act of 1973, 16 U.S.C. §§1531-1544

Under this sweeping piece of legislation, the U.S. government agreed to protect wildlife species that were in danger of becoming extinct by passing laws and establishing treaties that would make killing such animals a crime. Also, federally owned land that was considered critical to a species' survival would be preserved from development under the act, and all federal agencies and departments were obligated to establish practices that would help protect endangered wildlife.

Convention of International Trade in Endangered Species of Wildlife Fauna and Flora (1975)

This international treaty, commonly called CITES, controls the trade of endangered plants and animals across international borders in an effort to prevent the illegal sale of species on the brink of extinction. Today, the treaty covers more than 30,000 different species in 163 countries.

Humane Methods of Slaughter Act of 1978, 7 U.S.C. §§ 1901-1906

Often shortened as the "Humane Slaughter Act," this legislation was an important step in making slaughterhouse practices more humane. Congress asserted that every effort should be made during the slaughter process to prevent any unnecessary suffering of the animals. The act covers cattle and hogs, but not poultry. However, animals that are killed using ritual methods—most specifically, in preparing kosher foods for those of the Jewish faith—are exempt from this act. Although other religious faiths are not mentioned by name in the act, it is generally accepted that rituals performed in other cases, such as *halal* slaughter practiced by Muslims, are exempt as well.

State v. *Taub,* 11848-81 (1981), Maryland District Court unreported case

Dr. Edward Taub, head of the lab at the Institute for Behavioral Research in Silver Spring, Maryland, was found guilty on six counts of animal cruelty for not providing adequate care to his research monkeys. The case is significant as the first instance in which laboratory animal cruelty began to be taken seriously in the courtroom.

Taub v. *State*, 43 A.2d 819 (Md. 1983)

Dr. Taub appealed the earlier ruling in *State* v. *Taub* and in this case the judge ruled that the experiments on the monkeys were justified. Nevertheless, the case brought lab animal cruelty to the attention of the citizens of Maryland, and legislation was passed in the state that clarified what would be considered animal cruelty.

Food Security Act of 1985, 7 U.S.C. § 1631

The Food Security Act included a section called the Improved Standards for Laboratory Animals Act, which stated, among other things, that people handling animals in labs must be fully trained; it created Institutional Animal Care and Use Committees, strengthened standards for care, and mandated that dogs be exercised and better, more stimulating environments be available for primates.

Animal Enterprise Protection Act of 1992, 18 U.S.C. § 43

This law was passed as a reaction to the growing concern about acts of "terror" committed by groups such as the Animal Liberation Front. The law makes "animal enterprise terrorism"—defined as any act intended to cause "physical disruption to the functioning of an animal enterprise"—a federal crime. An animal enterprise is defined as any "commercial or academic enterprise that uses animals for food or fiber production, agriculture, research, or testing."

173

Lujan v. *Defenders of Wildlife,* 504 U.S. 555 (1992)
Considered the definitive decision on what merits legal standing for animals, this case involved the Environmental Protection Agency, which was failing to require that overseas business projects in which federal agencies were involved were not endangering native wildlife. The U.S. Supreme Court eventually ruled against the Defenders of Wildlife, saying that the plaintiffs lacked legal standing. The case has often been cited in subsequent lawsuits involving animal rights.

Twenty-Eight Hour Law of 1994, 49 U.S.C. § 80502
Designed so that farm animals are transported in ways that cause them less stress, this law says that these animals must be given time to rest at least once every twenty-eight hours while they are being transported to any location.

Recreational Hunting Safety and Preservation Act of 1994, 16 U.S.C. §§ 48
Commonly known as the "Hunter's Rights Amendment," this legislation prevents people from obstructing "a lawful hunt" in any way. Violating the law can result in a $10,000 fine if hunt saboteurs threaten or harm a hunter or his or her property.

American Legal Defense Fund v. *Espy I*, 23 F.3d 496 (D.C. Cir. 1994)
The American Legal Defense Fund (ALDF) challenged the exclusion of mice, rats, and birds from the Animal Welfare Act. In *ALDF* v. *Espy I* the court made a decision contrary to the conclusions drawn in the earlier *ALDF* v. *Yeutter* and *ALDF* v. *Madigan* cases, in which it was ruled that excluding these species was against the spirit of the AWA, because, as established in *Lujan*, the animals did not have legal standing because their danger was not imminent or impending.

American Legal Defense Fund v. *Espy II,* 29 F.3d 720 (D.C. Cir. 1994)
This lawsuit was instigated by the ALDF's dissatisfaction with the U.S. Department of Agriculture, which was neglecting to set minimum standards for the psychological welfare of animals in labs, zoos, circuses, and at animal dealer facilities. The court ruled that the USDA had, indeed, failed to create these requirements as mandated by Congress in 1985. However, on appeal, this decision was overturned because the animals involved were not considered to have legal standing.

Animal Legal Defense Fund v. *Glickman I,* 154 F.3d 426 (D.C. Cir. 1998)
Because *Lujan* v. *Defenders of Wildlife* made it so difficult to prove legal standing in cases involving animal rights where those filing suits could not show they were directly affected by the defendants' acts against animals, the ALDF decided to file a suit that involved animals on exhibits, such as zoos and circuses, where treatment of animals could negatively affect the public (specifically, paying customers of an enterprise) more directly. The lawsuit contended that the conditions of primates maintained at the Long Island Game Farm Park and Zoo were so substandard as to cause "aesthetic injury" to people observing the animals. Further, the injury was the result of the USDA's failure to enforce minimum care standards for these animals. The judges in the case ruled 7–4 in favor of the plaintiff that the ALDF did, indeed, have legal standing in the case.

Animal Legal Defense Fund* v. *Glickman II, 204 F.3d 229 (D.C. Cir. 2000)
  ALDF v. *Glickman I* established only that the plaintiff had legal standing in the case. In *ALDF* v. *Glickman II*, the ALDF actually sued Daniel Glickman, the secretary of the USDA, asserting that the regulations established by his office were not lawful because they did not protect the psychological well-being of the primates at the Long Island Game Farm Park and Zoo. This time, however, the judges ruled in favor of the defendant, saying that the regulations were consistent with the intentions of the Animal Welfare Act.

Terms and Concepts

animal husbandry

anthrocentrism

anthropomorphism

Creationism

Darwinism

endangered species

ethology

euthanasia

extinction

factory farm

genetic research

inbreeding

in silico

in vitro

in vivo

Social Darwinism

speciesism

theory of evolution

vivisection

xenotransplantation

Beginning Legal Research

The goal of POINT/COUNTERPOINT is not only to provide the reader with an introduction to a controversial issue affecting society, but also to encourage the reader to explore the issue more fully. This appendix, then, is meant to serve as a guide to the reader in researching the current state of the law as well as exploring some of the public-policy arguments as to why existing laws should be changed or new laws are needed.

Like many types of research, legal research has become much faster and more accessible with the invention of the Internet. This appendix discusses some of the best starting points, but of course "surfing the Net" will uncover endless additional sources of information—some more reliable than others. Some important sources of law are not yet available on the Internet, but these can generally be found at the larger public and university libraries. Librarians usually are happy to point patrons in the right direction.

The most important source of law in the United States is the Constitution. Originally enacted in 1787, the Constitution outlines the structure of our federal government and sets limits on the types of laws that the federal government and state governments can pass. Through the centuries, a number of amendments have been added to or changed in the Constitution, most notably the first ten amendments, known collectively as the Bill of Rights, which guarantee important civil liberties. Each state also has its own constitution, many of which are similar to the U.S. Constitution. It is important to be familiar with the U.S. Constitution because so many of our laws are affected by its requirements. State constitutions often provide protections of individual rights that are even stronger than those set forth in the U.S. Constitution.

Within the guidelines of the U.S. Constitution, Congress—both the House of Representatives and the Senate—passes bills that are either vetoed or signed into law by the President. After the passage of the law, it becomes part of the United States Code, which is the official compilation of federal laws. The state legislatures use a similar process, in which bills become law when signed by the state's governor. Each state has its own official set of laws, some of which are published by the state and some of which are published by commercial publishers. The U.S. Code and the state codes are an important source of legal research; generally, legislators make efforts to make the language of the law as clear as possible.

However, reading the text of a federal or state law generally provides only part of the picture. In the American system of government, after the legislature passes laws and the executive (U.S. President or state governor) signs them, it is up to the judicial branch of the government, the court system, to interpret the laws and decide whether they violate any provision of the Constitution. At the state level, each state's supreme court has the ultimate authority in determining what a law means and whether or not it violates the state constitution. However, the federal courts—headed by the U.S. Supreme Court—can review state laws and court decisions to determine whether they violate federal laws or the U.S. Constitution. For example, a state court may find that a particular criminal law is valid under the state's constitution, but a federal court may then review the state court's decision and determine that the law is invalid under the U.S. Constitution.

It is important, then, to read court decisions when doing legal research. The Constitution uses language that is intentionally very general—for example, prohibiting "unreasonable searches and seizures" by the police—and court cases often provide more guidance. For example, the U.S. Supreme Court's 2001 decision in *Kyllo* v. *United States* held that scanning the outside of a person's house using a heat sensor to determine whether the person is growing marijuana is unreasonable—*if* it is done without a search warrant secured from a judge. Supreme Court decisions provide the most definitive explanation of the law of the land, and it is therefore important to include these in research. Often, when the Supreme Court has not decided a case on a particular issue, a decision by a federal appeals court or a state supreme court can provide guidance; but just as laws and constitutions can vary from state to state, so can federal courts be split on a particular interpretation of federal law or the U.S. Constitution. For example, federal appeals courts in Louisiana and California may reach opposite conclusions in similar cases.

Lawyers and courts refer to statutes and court decisions through a formal system of citations. Use of these citations reveals which court made the decision (or which legislature passed the statute) and when and enables the reader to locate the statute or court case quickly in a law library. For example, the legendary Supreme Court case *Brown* v. *Board of Education* has the legal citation 347 U.S. 483 (1954). At a law library, this 1954 decision can be found on page 483 of volume 347 of the U.S. Reports, the official collection of the Supreme Court's decisions. Citations can also be helpful in locating court cases on the Internet.

Understanding the current state of the law leads only to a partial understanding of the issues covered by the POINT/COUNTERPOINT series. For a fuller understanding of the issues, it is necessary to look at public-policy arguments that the current state of the law is not adequately addressing the issue. Many groups lobby for new legislation or changes to existing legislation; the National Rifle Association (NRA), for example, lobbies Congress and the state legislatures constantly to make existing gun control laws less restrictive and not to pass additional laws. The NRA and other groups dedicated to various causes might also intervene in pending court cases: a group such as Planned Parenthood might file a brief *amicus curiae* (as "a friend of the court") — called an "amicus brief" — in a lawsuit that could affect abortion rights. Interest groups also use the media to influence public opinion, issuing press releases and frequently appearing in interviews on news programs and talk shows. The books in POINT/COUNTERPOINT list some of the interest groups that are active in the issue at hand, but in each case there are countless other groups working at the local, state, and national levels. It is important to read everything with a critical eye, for sometimes interest groups present information in a way that can be read only to their advantage. The informed reader must always look for bias.

Finding sources of legal information on the Internet is relatively simple thanks to "portal" sites such as FindLaw (*www.findlaw.com*), which provides access to a variety of constitutions, statutes, court opinions, law review articles, news articles, and other resources — including all Supreme Court decisions issued since 1893. Other useful sources of information include the U.S. Government Printing Office (*www.gpo.gov*), which contains a complete copy of the U.S. Code, and the Library of Congress's THOMAS system (*thomas.loc.gov*), which offers access to bills pending before Congress as well as recently passed laws. Of course, the Internet changes every second of every day, so it is best to do some independent searching. Most cases, studies, and opinions that are cited or referred to in public debate can be found online — and *everything* can be found in one library or another.

The Internet can provide a basic understanding of most important legal issues, but not all sources can be found there. To find some documents it is necessary to visit the law library of a university or a public law library; some cities have public law libraries, and many library systems keep legal documents at the main branch. On the following page are some common citation forms.

COMMON CITATION FORMS

Source of Law	Sample Citation	Notes
U.S. Supreme Court	*Employment Division v. Smith*, 485 U.S. 660 (1988)	The U.S. Reports is the official record of Supreme Court decisions. There is also an unofficial Supreme Court ("S.Ct.") reporter.
U.S. Court of Appeals	*United States v. Lambert*, 695 F.2d 536 (11th Cir.1983)	Appellate cases appear in the Federal Reporter, designated by "F." The 11th Circuit has jurisdiction in Alabama, Florida, and Georgia.
U.S. District Court	*Carillon Importers, Ltd. v. Frank Pesce Group, Inc.*, 913 F.Supp. 1559 (S.D.Fla.1996)	Federal trial-level decisions are reported in the Federal Supplement ("F.Supp."). Some states have multiple federal districts; this case originated in the Southern District of Florida.
U.S. Code	Thomas Jefferson Commemoration Commission Act, 36 U.S.C., §149 (2002)	Sometimes the popular names of legislation—names with which the public may be familiar—are included with the U.S. Code citation.
State Supreme Court	*Sterling v. Cupp*, 290 Ore. 611, 614, 625 P.2d 123, 126 (1981)	The Oregon Supreme Court decision is reported in both the state's reporter and the Pacific regional reporter.
State statute	Pennsylvania Abortion Control Act of 1982, 18 Pa. Cons. Stat. 3203-3220 (1990)	States use many different citation formats for their statutes.

page:

16: Associated Press, AP

54: Courtesy of the Animal Welfare
Report, 2001

Cover: Associated Press, AP

122: Associated Press, AP

190: © Constance Wardell

KEVIN HILE is a freelance editor and writer from Michigan, where he lives with his wife, Janet. After graduating from Adrian College in 1988, he worked for ten years as an editor for the Gale Group, producing books for a number of library reference series, as well as

a CD-ROM project. He was then employed briefly by ACMedia, a publisher of college financial aid and travel guides; this was followed by two years as a Website content director for American Collegiate Marketing. In 2002, he decided to go freelance. Hile has written for and edited projects on a wide variety of subjects, including literary biography, science, film, education, college financing, career opportunities, employment, travel, entertainment, and juvenile crime. His biggest passion, however, is wildlife conservation, and he currently volunteers at Potter Park Zoo in Lansing, Michigan. He is also the author of Chelsea House's *Trial of Juveniles as Adults* and an as-yet unpublished fantasy novel.

ALAN MARZILLI, of Durham, North Carolina, is an independent consultant working on several ongoing projects for state and federal government agencies and nonprofit organizations. He has spoken about mental health issues in more than twenty states, the District of Columbia, and Puerto Rico; his work includes training mental health administrators, nonprofit management and staff, and people with mental illness and their family members on a wide variety of topics, including effective advocacy, community-based mental health services, and housing. He has written several handbooks and training curricula that are used nationally. He managed statewide and national mental health advocacy programs and worked for several public interest lobbying organizations in Washington, D.C., while studying law at Georgetown University.